A Chronicle of Herbs

THIS NOBLE HARVEST

A Chronicle of Herbs

THIS NOBLE HARVEST

BY ANNE OPHELIA DOWDEN

Illustrated by the Author

COLLINS
New York and Cleveland

PLANTS SHOWN ON THE JACKET
Borage, *Borago officinalis*
Chamomile, *Anthemis nobilis*
Poppy, *Papaver somniferum*

PLANTS SHOWN ON THE TITLE PAGE
Florentine iris, *Iris germanica* var. *florentina*
Autumn crocus, *Colchicum autumnale*
Christmas rose, *Helleborus niger*
Scilla, *Endymion non-scriptus*

PLANTS IN BOUQUET OF FRAGRANT HERBS
Sweet violet, *Viola odorata*
Lavender, *Lavandula officinalis*
Southernwood, *Artemisia abrotanum*
Lemon verbena, *Lippia citriodora*
Costmary, *Chrysanthemum balsamita*
Geraniums, *Geranium spp.*

All plants pictured in this book—
except enlarged details—are exactly 7/8 natural size.

Library of Congress Cataloging in Publication Data
Dowden, Anne Ophelia Todd, 1907- This noble harvest.
Includes index.
SUMMARY: An introduction to herbs, their history,
characteristics, and their many uses.
1. Herbs—Juvenile literature. 2. Herbs (in religion, folklore,
etc.)—Juvenile literature. 3. Plants, Useful—Juvenile literature.
[1. Herbs. 2. Herbs (in religion, folklore, etc.)] I. Title.
SB351.H5D67 635'.7 79-12021
ISBN 0-529-05548-1

Published by William Collins Publishers, Inc.
Cleveland and New York, 1979.

Manufactured in the United States of America.

ACKNOWLEDGMENTS

In the preparation of this book, many people have helped, with both gathering information and gathering the plants whose portraits I have painted. Most of these plants and much information came from Mrs. Gertrude Foster, editor of The Herb Grower, Falls Village, Connecticut, who once collaborated with me on a projected book that never materialized.

In my pursuit of history and legend, I was aided by a number of wonderfully efficient librarians: Miss Elizabeth Hall and Miss Carolyn Oates of the Horticultural Society of New York; Miss Marie Giasi at the Brooklyn Botanic Garden; and Mrs. Evelyn W. Semler at the Morgan Library. Mr. Frank J. Anderson, Honorary Curator of Rare Books at the New York Botanical Garden, opened that collection to me and gave his expert knowledge of the ancient herbals and hours of his time in helping locate appropriate woodcut illustrations.

I am also indebted to Dr. Peter K. Nelson, Department of Biology, Brooklyn College, for his careful reading of my manuscript; to Dr. Alden G. Vaughan, Hanover, New Hampshire, for translation of some passages of medieval Latin; and to my husband, Raymond B. Dowden, for his practical assistance and discerning critical advice.

This bouquet of fragrant herbs is gratefully offered to
Gertrude B. Foster,
herbalist, friend, and mistress of a happy garden,
who generously shares with me her knowledge,
her enthusiasm, and her plants.

CONTENTS

Acknowledgments

1. A TREASURE OF HERBES 9
2. SCIENCE NOBLY SUPPORTED 14
3. THE FRIEND OF PHYSICIANS 21
4. ENCHANTED HERBS 38
5. THE GRACE THAT LIES IN HERBS 48
6. GOOD HUSWIVES DELIGHT 51
7. THE PRAISE OF COOKS 65

Uses of Herbs in Cooking 73
Plant Families of Herbs 75
Some Books About Herbs 77
Index 78

A MEDIEVAL HERB GARDEN
Brunschwig: *Liber de Arte Distillandi,* Strassburg, 1500

A TREASURE OF HERBES

The story of herbs is the story of people. For half a million years, herbs have shared the daily life of men and women. They have both shaped and mirrored every step of human development, and they have traveled with civilization as it spread around the world. Human beings owe their very existence to plants. The leafy world, in addition to providing most of the oxygen we breathe, has since the dim ages of prehistory given us food, clothing, and shelter; medicines, dyes, and fragrances; pens, paper, and cosmetics. Plants have nourished and sustained us, inspired our dreams and our religions and sent men out on voyages across the seas.

From lofty trees to humble mosses, thousands of plants have contributed to our welfare, in hundreds of different ways. Some of these useful plants are called "herbs." Others are not, and the use of that word is not always logical. For botanists, an herb is a soft or nonwoody plant — one that usually dies back to the ground after each growing season — and a botanist's herbs include a great part of the vegetation of the earth. On the other hand, there are people who use the word solely for plants that provide medicines and flavorings. So one cannot say precisely

what makes an herb an herb. Perhaps it is best to think of herbs loosely as all those useful plants that have most intimately shared people's day-to-day activities—those plants grown and used at home rather than in industry or agriculture. They would also include many plants gathered in the wild and exclude the spices that come mostly from Oriental trees. Almost to the present day, human beings would have found life without these homely plants difficult and uncomfortable at best, and at worst, impossible.

The herbs that provide for so many varied needs must, of course, possess varied qualities, which can be as different as the toughness of their fibers or the color yielded by their roots, but

From Roman times, elecampane root was used for sweets and medicine, and it is still an ingredient in absinthe. Applied primarily to bronchial ills, it was also "good for wagging teeth." Valerian has an alkaloid in its rhizomes, an alkaloid that affects the cerebrospinal system, and was widely used in England for overwrought nerves during air raids. Cats love it as they do catnip.

by far the greatest number are fragrant or pleasant-tasting. These aromatic herbs occur in many plant families, and they are especially common in three: the Mint family, the Carrot family, the Composite family. Their scent and taste come mostly from volatile oils, produced not by the flowers but by glandular hairs or corky cells in the leaves. These oils are released when the plant is crushed and warmed in the hand. If the cell walls are not broken, the oils will not escape, and the flavor can be preserved indefinitely by drying. Botanists are not sure what value such oils have for the plants: perhaps they attract pollinating insects or repel grazing animals. In the arid countries where so many herbs are native, survival is hard, and any plant is better off if it is distasteful to animals and covered with hairs to protect it from the sun. Many herbs have "fur" so dense that the leaves and stems look like silver velvet.

This adds to the beauty of an herb garden, which often depends on foliage masses of many textures and tints, ranging from feathery to coarse, from pale silver to rich green to purple. Since herbs are grown mainly for their leaves, roots, or seeds, flowers are always of secondary importance; and many herb blossoms are small and inconspicuous, like those of most mints and all artemisias. But there are dramatic exceptions — iris, poppy, peony, chicory, elecampane, and others — all large enough and bright enough to shine as brightly in the floral border as in the kitchen garden.

The names of herbs can be a story in themselves, and they tell us as much about people as about plants. The *wort* that occurs over and over in such names as liverwort and St. John's wort is the early Anglo-Saxon word for "plant." Liverwort has liver-shaped leaves, and St. John's wort was dedicated to St. John because it is in bloom on his feast day. Valerian comes from the Latin *valeo,* meaning "I am well." Henbane and wolfsbane were the bane, or poison, of poultry (accidentally) and of wolves (intentionally). The scientific names also describe the use or appearance of a plant. *Tussilago* (coltsfoot) comes from *tussis,* Latin for "cough;" and *digitalis* (foxglove) means "of the finger." The common species name *officinalis* (as in *Salvia officinalis*) tells us that the bearer of it was once "official" or medicinal.

Long before plants received these names, they were shaping the lives of men and women, beginning to determine the patterns that civilization would follow. We can only imagine the prehistoric groping by which primitive people slowly learned all that plants could do for them. In the beginning, human beings lived as animals do, eating nuts and berries in addition to the game they were able to kill. Millennia passed while they tried things out, noted successes and failures, passed information on from generation to generation, and gradually discovered what they could eat or smoke or rub on a wound. They did this timidly, fearful of the spirits they believed were in the plants, fearful, in fact, of all the forces of nature, which seemed to represent gods or demons. Plants were always treated with respect; nearly all of them were gathered with a prayer, and some could be collected only by priests or magicians.

They were at first picked wherever they happened to grow, by people who were primarily roving hunters. Finally someone made the important discovery that he could cultivate his own plants and grow them where he wished. No step on the road to civilization was more momentous than this. It changed the wandering hunters into settled farmers and brought a stability that eventually made possible the growth of cities and the development of learning. Once plants were under their control, farmers and gardeners began to accumulate information about them; and over the succeeding centuries, they joined the gatherers of wild herbs — from the Greek rhizomati to nineteenth-century American doctors—in contributing bit by bit to a vast body of herbal knowledge. Assembled purely for utility, this herbal lore became the foundation for all modern botany and most modern medicine.

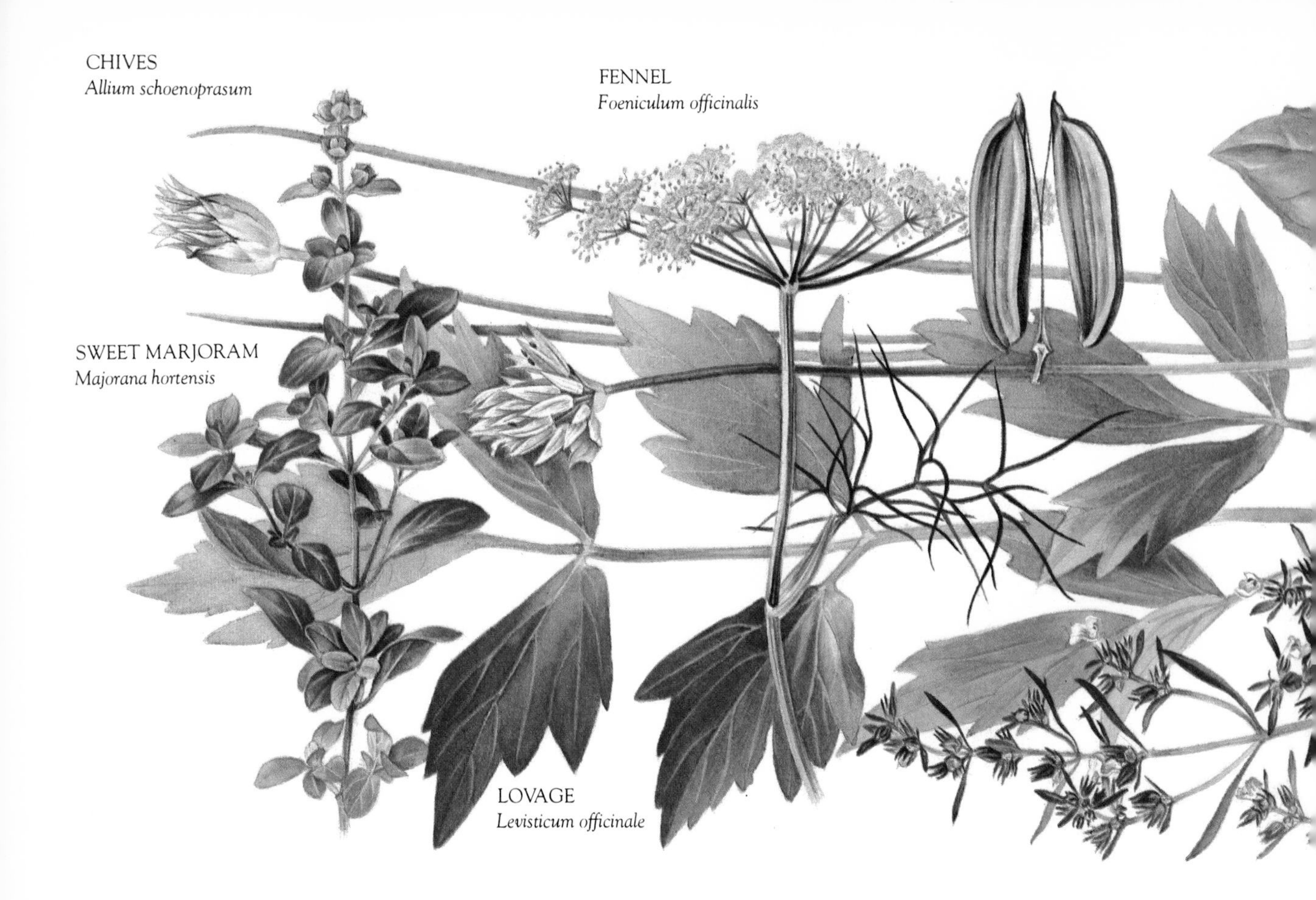

SCIENCE NOBLY SUPPORTED

Almost as soon as man could write at all, he wrote about herbs. He was doing it three thousand years before Christ in China, India, Sumer, and Egypt. China and India contributed only a little to our herbal heritage, but the countries surrounding the Mediterranean bestowed on us an enormous wealth of knowledge, as well as most of the plants we have used for so many centuries.

At the eastern end of the Mediterranean almost five thousand years ago, plant remedies were recorded on Sumerian clay tablets and in the Egyptian Ebers Papyrus, which mentions nearly seven hundred herbs. A few centuries later—between 2100 and 1500 B.C.—Minoans on the island of Crete

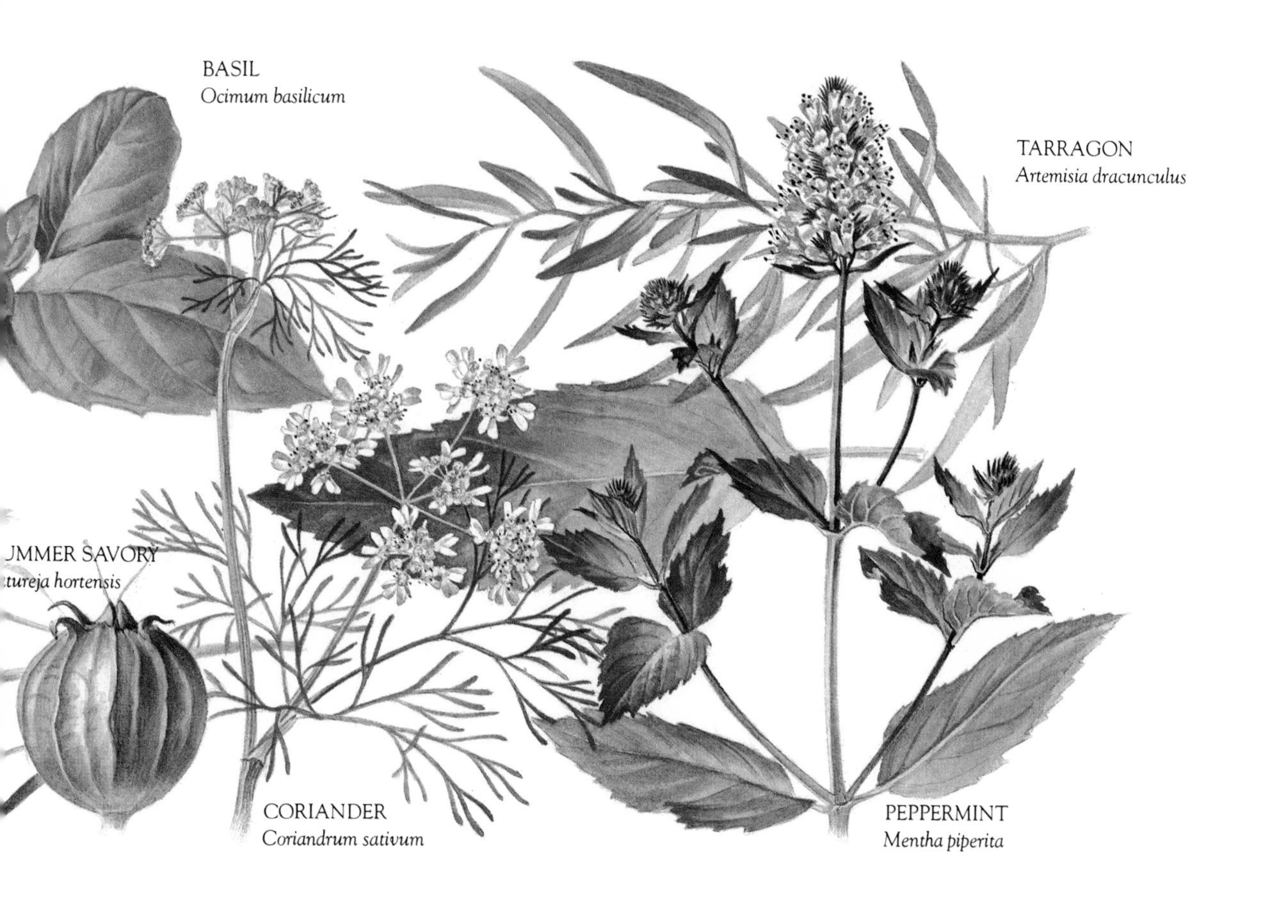

painted our earliest pictures of flowers, first on decorated pottery jars and then on beautifully frescoed walls.

Another early record of plants is on the wall of an Egyptian temple. In 1478 B.C. King Thutmose III returned triumphant from conquests in Syria, bringing among the spoils of his campaign a remarkable collection of trees and herbs. They were planted in a courtyard of the great temple at Karnak, and their pictures and descriptions were recorded in bas-relief sculpture on the temple wall — the first botanical textbook. Five hundred years later, King Solomon wrote books about plants and magic, but they were lost—probably destroyed "lest their contents should do harm."

It was in Greece, however, that our scientific knowledge of plants really began. Many Greeks investigated the natural world, and many wrote about herbs and medicine, but Theophrastus, pupil of Aristotle, was the true father of botany. In his *Enquiry into Plants,* written in the fourth century B.C., he described five hundred different plants, with their medical uses. Even earlier than that, the physician Hippocrates treated his patients with four hundred herbs, more than half of which remained in use until modern synthetics replaced them.

The Romans, on the other hand, were not researchers, even though they were fine gardeners who grew and used hundreds of herbs in cooking and medicine. When they wrote about plants, it was usually only to pass along the words of the earlier Greek authors. The famous *Natural History* of Pliny the Elder is a vast hodgepodge of such material gathered from two thousand manuscripts, along with much sensible gardening advice and a great deal of amusing superstition. Thus the Romans' chief contribution to botany was the spreading of existing knowledge—and spreading of the plants themselves—over all the wide area they conquered. England, for instance, first received the ancient Mediterranean herbs from the Romans. (The plants mostly died out, however, and had to be reintroduced by St. Augustine and his monks.)

Nevertheless, it was a Roman citizen who compiled the most influential *Materia Medica,* or medical herb book, the world has known. Dioscorides was born in Asia Minor and educated in Greece, but he traveled widely as a physician with the Roman armies. About A.D. 50 he wrote the book that remained the basis of herbal medicine for more than a thousand years.

After the fall of the Roman Empire, the center of civilization moved to the East, and it was Arab physicians who preserved and used the works of the Greeks. Accompanying the Saracen armies around the Mediterranean, they spread this knowledge as far as Spain, adding their own discoveries, especially the art of distilling. In Europe during those centuries, herbal lore, like most other knowledge, would have been totally lost if it had not been preserved in the monasteries. Plants necessary for healing were grown by the monks in their "physick gardens" and administered by the same monks with the guidance of Dioscorides' herbal. Few plants were grown for any but medicinal uses, and none at all for pleasure. To earn its place in the garden, a plant had to be "good for something."

During these so-called Dark Ages, there was one glimmer of light outside the monasteries—the reign of Charlemagne, from A.D. 768 to 814. This remarkable monarch was interested not only in war and conquest, but also in the minute details of life throughout his domain. He issued long and complicated directives about the running of his estates, among which are rules for managing farms and vineyards and a list of all the plants to be grown there. It includes about seventy-five herbs and vegetables we use today.

In the centuries after Charlemagne, life gradually changed; knowledge of the virtues of plants spread outside the monastery walls, and gardens became more and more a part of everyday life. In the villages, there were herb gatherers and wise women to provide special cures and charms. In the towns, drugs were sold in market booths; and doctors and apothecaries grew, distilled, and applied their own medicines.

But the most important "doctors" were the gentlewomen who presided over large households. They were expected to "helpe their owne family and their poore neighbours" and to "take much paines both to doe good unto them and to plant those herbes that are conducing to their desires." These women

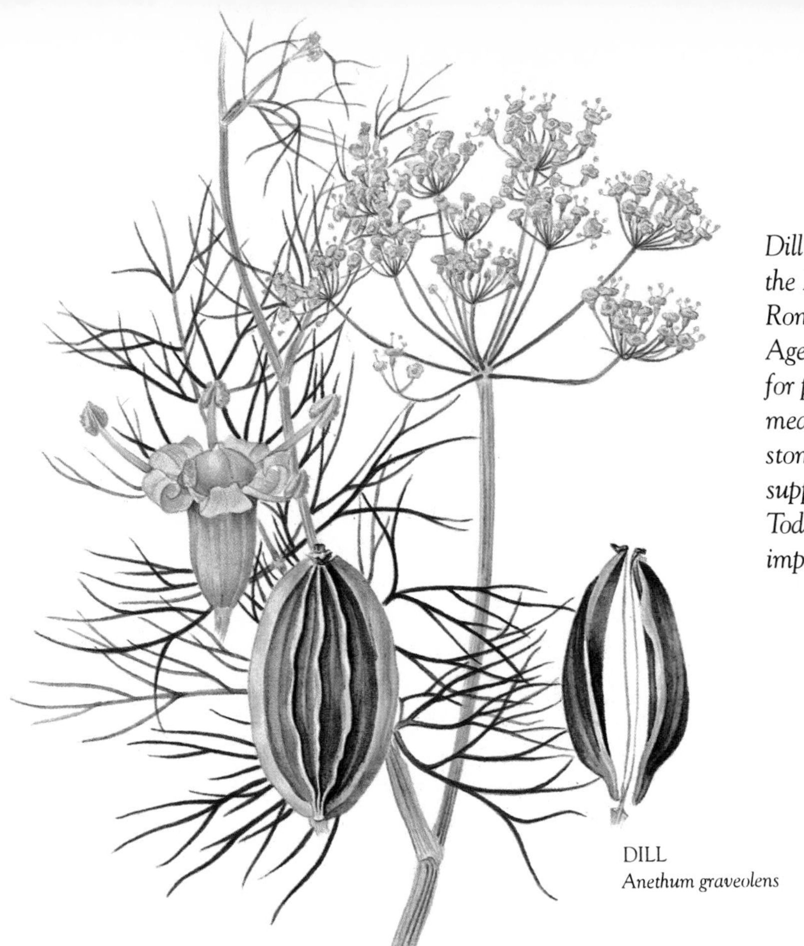

Dill is an ancient herb, tithed by the Pharisees, well known to the Romans, a favorite in the Middle Ages. Used against witchcraft and for perfuming soap, it was also a medicine for "wicked winds in the stomach." Boiled in wine, it was supposed to excite the passions. Today its seeds and leaves are an important flavoring.

DILL
Anethum graveolens

bore a heavy responsibility—they had to diagnose and treat every ailment from a sore throat to the plague, and they directed the making of all medicines and many other household necessities. From about the fifteenth century on, every household had a stillroom, used originally for distilling medicines and cordials, but eventually for all kinds of special cookery, like making cosmetics, soaps, and candies. Every housewife had a stillroom book, in which she kept recipes handed down by her family or collected from her friends. These books were much more important than a modern cook's file of recipes. Between their lines, we can read the story of all the daily problems a household had to solve, and they give us fascinating and valuable knowledge of the way people lived from the fifteenth to the eighteenth centuries.

The outstanding quality of marsh-mallow is its thick, slimy juice, valued since Biblical times for soothing and healing both the inside and the outside of the body. It was often used in a paste to protect the hands of those who had to undergo the medieval ordeal of holding a red-hot iron. Marshmallow no longer has any connection with the candy of the same name.

MARSHMALLOW
Althaea officinalis

During all the Middle Ages, as herbs were used, books about them continued to appear, all copied and recopied—by hand of course — from a few standard early works, especially that of Dioscorides. No one wrote anything original about plants until the Renaissance dawned, with its spirit of inquiry and its invention of printing. (Even the first printed books were merely new versions of the same ancient manuscripts.) Then, in every country of Europe, men began to look at the plants around them with a new curiosity and a broader point of view, and to question and test their long-sacred medical traditions. Their descriptions of plants were fresh and new, and they ushered in the age of the great herbals, which reached their height in seventeenth-century England.

"Herbal" is a rather indefinite term. It refers primarily to a collection of plant descriptions put together for medical purposes, but the early herbals contain a good bit of magic and superstition, and the late ones tell a lot about gardening. Some, like the *Hortus Sanitatis* of 1491, are a sort of medieval natural history, describing animals and minerals as well as plants. Great authors like William Turner in the sixteenth century and John Gerard and John Parkinson at the beginning of the seventeenth, wrote herbals that were intended as medical treatises, but that reveal the writers' great delight in plants and interest in growing them. Slightly later, Nicholas Culpeper put out a popular herbal much influenced by the wave of astrology then prevalent in England. Until the seventeenth century at least, science and magic competed to dominate men's minds, but out of the herbals came scientific botany, as chemistry came out of alchemy. Though these books give us important information about every aspect of daily life, their record of the medical uses of herbs is unquestionably the most important part of this information and the most far-reaching in its consequences.

THE FRIEND OF PHYSICIANS

Almost every plant that grows has somewhere been considered a cure for something; and for centuries no botanist ever described a plant without adding a list of ailments it might cure, for "God and nature made nothing in vain." The search for such cures was part of our primitive ancestors' very earliest experiments; and by the time they were able to shape weapons and tools—about 17,000 years ago—they were probably also treating illnesses and injuries with simple herbal remedies.

They undoubtedly treated their ailments with magic. Primitive people did not understand disease. They believed that it came, not from natural causes, but from evil influences exerted by gods or demons or other human beings, which could be combatted only with stronger magic and divine aid. This idea persisted for centuries—long after there was real knowledge of the human body and how it works. So the use of herbs was only a part of therapy that involved charms and rituals and was at first performed chiefly by priests. In ancient Greece, people went to temples in groves sacred to the god Aesculapius, hoping to be healed by his priests. In northern Europe, the Druids served as both priests and physicians, and so did the medicine men of the American Indians.

By the time of the Egyptians and the Greeks, the early healers had, by trial and error, compiled a list of "simples"—herbs used as basic medicinal ingredients. Once discovered, many of these simples were used continuously over the centuries, alone or in combination. There were hundreds of them (Theophrastus, as we know, described five hundred, and the Saxons also had five hundred), and they included nearly all our well-known cooking herbs as well as such plants as coltsfoot,

Rue, which is sometimes the cause of a severe skin rash, had a limited use in cooking; but it was supposed to give second sight and to sharpen wit, and sprigs were worn in the stocking to drive off witches. It was planted with parsley as an edging for flower beds, so enterprises just beginning were said to be "at the parsley and the rue."

RUE
Ruta graveolens

elecampane, and clover. A great many of them were strongly aromatic or bitter in taste—qualities that seemed to recommend them as medicines.

Two of the most important simples were sage and rue. Sage was near the top of any medieval herb list. Walahfrid Strabo, about the time of Charlemagne, wrote "it holds the place of honor, is of good scent, and virtues for many ills." These ills included almost every ailment that man is heir to: indigestion, palsy, bad nerves, "abortments," toothache, bad memory, the effects of poison, and many others—enough indeed, to inspire the old saying "How can a man die who grows sage in his garden?" The plant's scientific name, Salvia, comes from the Latin "to heal."

Sage was as important in cooking as in medicine. It was a potherb and a salad herb, and it still is a favorite seasoning for meat, especially pork and poultry. It was used in hand-washing water and as a strewing herb. Europeans drank sage tea before the introduction of China tea, and it was thought to soften grief and to promote long life.

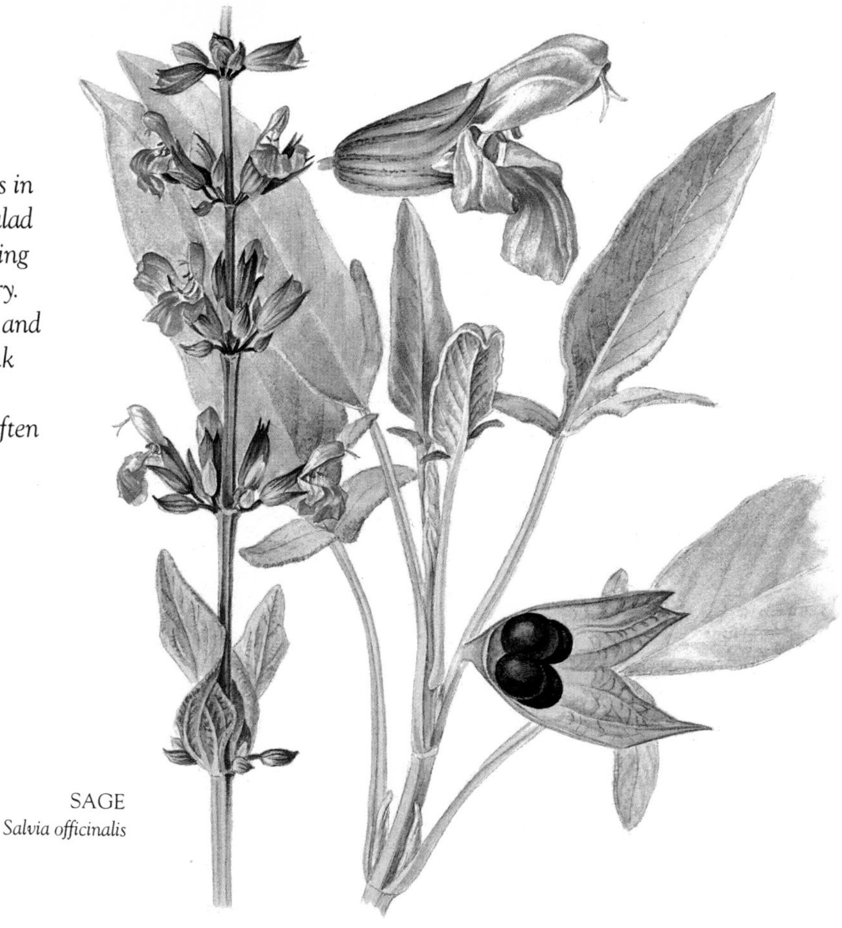

SAGE
Salvia officinalis

Rue, Shakespeare's "sour Herb of Grace," symbolized repentance, but it was also prescribed for rheumatism, worms, hysteria, colic, eye disease, and dumbness caused by spells. In fact, John Gerard gives a whole page to his list of its virtues. It was considered an antidote to poisons and snakebite; placed in a bed, it was expected to preserve chastity and, more reasonably, to kill bedbugs and fleas. Both sage and rue (along with eleven other herbs) were ingredients in the Vinegar of the Four Thieves, with which burglars anointed themselves as a protection when they robbed the houses of people who had died of the plague.

Today we find it amusing, and also a bit sad, that herbs like these two could be used so hopefully in so many unsuitable ways. But both of them contain substances—the volatile oil of sage and the rutin in rue—that have some effect on the human body. There were unquestionably many herbal remedies that provided nothing except much-needed vitamins, but herbal medicine was not mere nonsense any more than early medical practice in general was nonsense. For thousands of years, physicians dealt as best they could with the ever-present problems of illness and human suffering. Without the resources of modern science, they were often wrong about the functions of the body and the nature of disease. But each century added new discoveries, and all of today's medical knowledge had its origins in those early attempts at healing.

During those centuries, all medicines—except for a very few mineral and animal substances—came from plants; and even today, many of our medicines are synthesized versions of chemicals originally derived from plants. A large number of the ancient simples persisted into modern times. Early twentieth century pharmacopoeias listed nearly a hundred of them, including such plants as lily of the valley, which contains glucosides that stimulate the heart; and autumn crocus, which has colchinine, used for centuries in treating gout and recently as a means of producing new varieties of garden plants by altering their chromosome numbers.

A few of the ancient herbs were so effective that they are still important in medicine. Most of them are effective because their alkaloids and glucosides produce a powerful reaction in blood vessels or heart or nervous system. Correctly used, this action is a valuable medical tool; incorrectly used, it can kill. Even in early times, these very poisonous plants were generally employed only by specialists and not widely grown in home gardens. (A number of common herbs also are poisonous, and no one without expert knowledge should ever dose himself.)

DOCTOR IN APOTHECARY SHOP
Hortus Sanitatis,
Strassburg, c.1497

Belladonna, thorn apple, and henbane are such plants—all extremely poisonous, and all belonging to the same family as tomato, potato, and tobacco. Their leaves, roots, and seeds contain the narcotic alkaloids atropine and hyoscyamine, which work on the central nervous system. Belladonna is also called deadly nightshade, and its scientific name, *Atropa,* comes from one of the Three Fates — Atropos, who cut the thread of life. One herbalist called belladonna a "naughtie and

deadly plant," and Gerard advises us to "banish it from your gardens and the use of it also, being a plant so furious and deadly." The Scots under Macbeth, during a truce in their war with the Danes, served their adversaries beer with belladonna in it, then fell on their drugged victims and killed them. Until recently, it was prescribed for relief of spasms like those in asthma, and it is still used by eye specialists because of its action in dilating the pupil of the eye.

Henbane was used medicinally from remote times for its narcotic and sedative properties. Necklaces of the root were put on children in the hope they would prevent fits and make teething easier. In modern medicine, henbane is an ingredient in the drug that produces "twilight sleep" in childbirth; and

HENBANE
Hyoscyamus niger

Belladonna was so called because beautiful Italian ladies used it to dilate the pupils of their eyes. Thorn apple was used by the priests of Apollo at Delphi to assist in their prophecies. Its flowers open at night and are intensely fragrant to attract moths, but the plant as a whole has a nauseating odor. Henbane was considered by the ancients a plant of ill omen. They used it at funerals and on tombs, and believed that it was worn around the heads of the dead in Hades. The Assyrians placed it on door hinges to keep sorcery out of a house.

most wartime brain-washing involved hyoscyamine, plus scopalomine (from another plant of the same family) and morphine or a barbiturate. The scientific name *Hyoscyamus* means "hog-bean," because swine are supposed to eat it safely. It stupifies other animals, and its seeds, with those of thorn apple, were sometimes mixed with the fodder of horses and cows in the hope that placid animals would gain weight more quickly. Thorn apple, boiled in hog's grease, was widely used for burns and inflammations, and Parkinson approves it as a drink for "one that is to have a legge or an arme cut off." It is often called jimsonweed in the United States because it was first introduced near Jamestown, Virginia. Though this plant came to us from Europe, a similar species is native to South

America, where the Incas used it as an anesthetic, and a Colombian tribe gave it to wives and slaves before burying them alive with dead warriors.

The New World, in fact, contributed hundreds of new plants to the physick gardens and vegetable plots of Europe. In North America, though the first English colonists brought their herbs and their herb lore along with them, they also soon began to gather information from the Indians and to learn the virtues of the native plants that the Indians grew or collected in the wild. The Spanish conquerors of the Incas and Aztecs of Central and South America sent out their doctors along with their armies, and the priests who converted the Indians also learned native medicine. The private physician of Philip II of Spain spent a number of years in Mexico and recorded some three thousand Aztec herbal remedies. Many of these were no more effective than the traditional European herbs, but among them were such drugs as curare, quinine, cocaine, and tobacco (as well as some important vegetables like potato, tomato, corn, and squash.)

Even today, new herbal drugs are being discovered. Botanists are searching in remote parts of the world, just as the Spaniards did, looking into the magic and medicine of primitive tribes for possible new remedies. Not many years ago, rauwolfia, a plant used in folk medicine in India, was found to produce a drug that became the first important tranquilizer; and in the United States alone, its sales reached $20,000,000 a year. From wild lobelia, a small weed that clutters many gardens in the eastern United States, comes the alkaloid lobeline, recently used as a chemical aid in breaking the smoking habit. Among the hundreds of thousands of chemicals tested in the fight against cancer, two derived from the Madagascar periwinkle have proved promising.

In most cases, newly discovered plants go immediately to the laboratories of pharmaceutical chemists, where their active ingredients are separated out and synthesized, or reproduced by chemical means. Today, synthesis has "copied" nearly all the drugs that were once obtained only from living plants, because modern industry is impatient with the slowness and waste involved in growing (or collecting) and processing plants. And it is also true that the chemical content of synthetic drugs can be standardized and controlled in a way not possible with natural drugs. In nature, plant ingredients vary from day to day —even from morning to evening—and according to soil and climate; and the leaf of one digitalis plant could be much more potent than the leaf of another collected at another time or in another place.

But true herbal drugs are still used in homeopathic medicine, and in the 1975 United States *Pharmacopoeia* a handful of the ancient simples remain unsynthesized. Among them are the drugs opium, digitalis, belladonna, castor oil, and peppermint, and also a number of oils used in formulating medicines: anise, coriander, licorice, cotton, and sesame.

Digitalis and opium both come from plants that are as beautiful as they are medicinally potent—foxglove and poppy. The pink bells of foxglove were always considered fairies' flowers, but the old herbalists used its leaves to treat a variety of ailments not at all related either to fairies or to the plant's true area of effectiveness, the heart. Gerard, for instance, recommends it for stoppages of the liver or spleen, while other herbalists applied it to external sores and wounds. Actually, it contains four powerful glucosides, of which three are heart stimulants, so that it is now a standard drug in heart therapy. It has also been tried recently in the treatment of glaucoma and muscular dystrophy.

OPIUM POPPY
Papaver somniferum

In Greek legend, poppies crowned the twin gods of sleep and death. Seeds of the plant are not narcotic and have been used since prehistoric times in food and as a source of oil.

The history of opium is far more complicated and more interesting. The plant that produces it is familiar to everyone: the common garden poppy with smooth bluish leaves. Originally, its flowers were single rather than double, and white or lavender instead of red as they often are today. The skin of its unripe seed pod contains a milky juice from which is derived opium and its relatives, laudanum, morphine, codeine, and heroin.

Long before the dawn of history, men were aware of the poppy's narcotic qualities. It was used by Neolithic Swiss lake dwellers, and mentioned in Sumerian clay tablets. The Egyp-

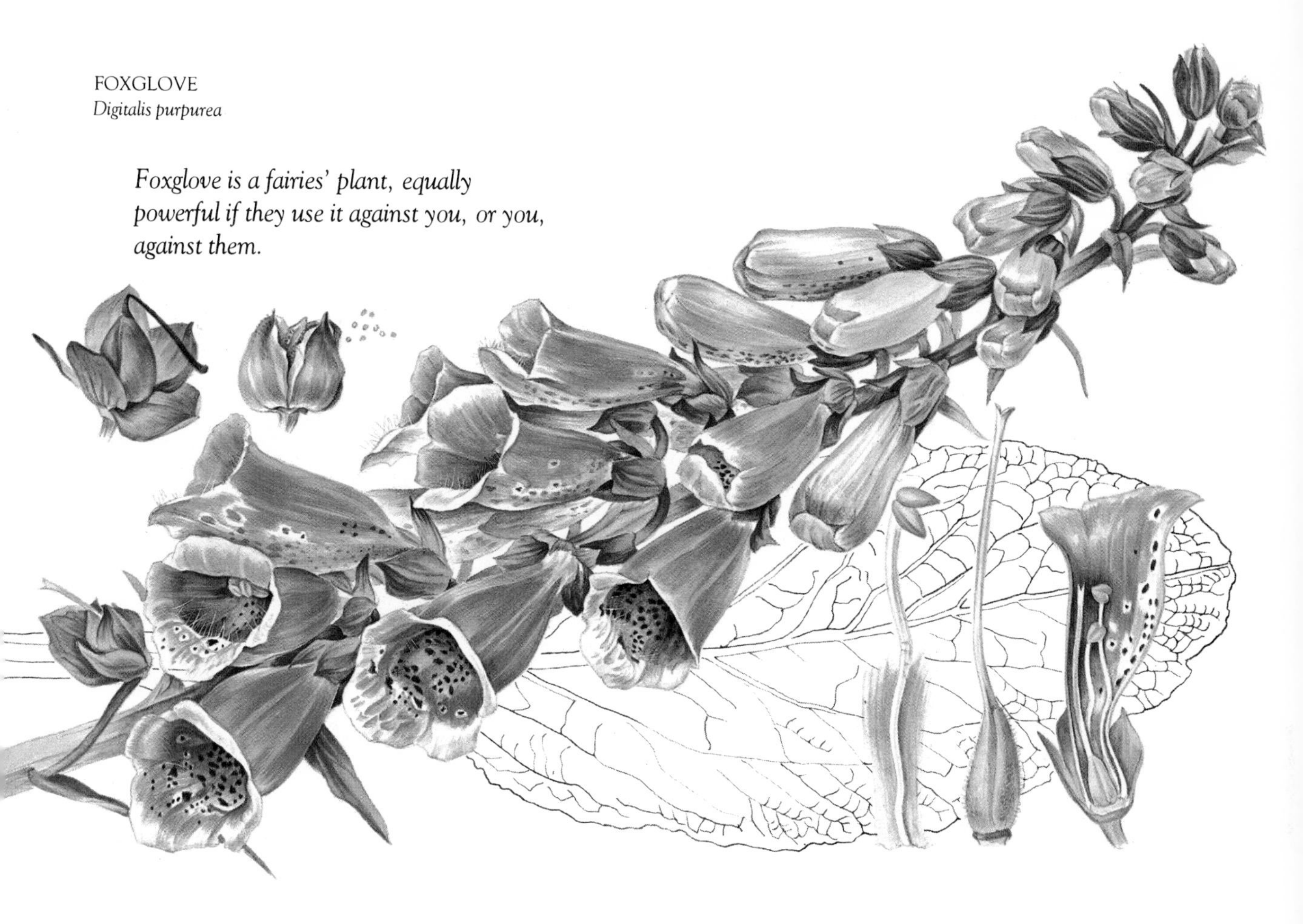

FOXGLOVE
Digitalis purpurea

Foxglove is a fairies' plant, equally powerful if they use it against you, or you, against them.

tians gave it to children who cried too much (as did other harassed mothers as late as 1900), and they also prescribed it for such ailments as pain in the abdomen and sore feet. Opium was important in Assyrian, Greek, and Roman medicine; and in Europe it became one of the most valued drugs, in spite of its known dangers. Gerard says it is "not to be used but in extreme necessitie, and that is when no other mitigator or assuager of paine doth anything prevaile." During all these centuries, it was used solely as a medicine, mostly for its sedative properties, but also as a physic and an astringent. Opium smoking, which probably originated in Persia, was not a European custom. But

WOMEN WORKING IN A STILL-ROOM
John Evelyn: *The French Gardener,*
London, 1672

almost inevitably, a drug so effective and so accessible eventually became a stock-in-trade of the medical quacks who flourished from the seventeenth century up until the Food and Drug Laws of the twentieth cut short their activities. As late as 1910, their patent medicines, as well as tincture of laudanum, could be bought as easily as aspirin is today, and opium became a social problem. However, in spite of its sinister side, opium has brought blessed relief from pain to men and women for hundreds of years. In a fourteenth-century manuscript, there is a prescription for a drink "to make a man sleep while men carve him." It includes several narcotics—poison hemlock, bryony, henbane, and poppy—boiled in the gall of a boar.

All medicinal plants, of course—no matter how authentic their virtues — were used sometimes in fantastic and even dangerous ways. The history of herbal medicine, as of all medicine, is intertwined with magic, alchemy, and the occult. In fact, we can scarcely tell where medicine leaves off and magic begins, since most magic plants have at least a few therapeutic chemicals, and most true medicines have been used in superstitious ways or applied to ailments for which they have no value. In ancient times, every conceivable illness had its herbal cure. And there were also herbs for the bites of leopards and dragons, mad dogs and scorpions; for nightmares and melancholy and falling hair; and for getting rid of "proud and superfluous flesh." Since disease was often believed to be caused by creatures of darkness, spells and incantations were an important part of many treatments. Some herbs were worn or carried rather than swallowed; many were swallowed to the accompaniment of a charm; and nearly all were thought to owe their powers to the position of the sun and moon at the time of gathering. There was a general belief, even two hundred years ago, that every plant was under the influence of a particular planet and "if it be not gathered according to the rules of astrology, it hath little or no virtue in it."

Some "medicinal herbs" were much better magic than medicine — actually so useless that one wonders how they gained their reputations. Betony, for instance, written about in Augustus Caesar's day, was grown in monastery gardens, and was accorded second highest place among all the hundreds of simples. It was said to be a cure for forty-seven disorders,

COMFREY
Symphytum caucasicum

Comfrey has been used chiefly as a medicine, though its young leaves and blanched shoots were sometimes eaten. Its leaves and roots have a slippery juice, valued as a softener in poultices and sometimes still used in cosmetics. Betony was worn as an amulet to drive away fearful visions, devils, and despair. The Egyptians and Romans esteemed horehound, chiefly as a medicine, but also as a protection against magic. Lavender flowers were often put in wine, and in Italy were a charm against the evil eye.

among which were "elf-sickness" and witches' spells, ailments over which it may have had the power it completely lacked in ailments of the body. Though betony is now discredited, lavender and horehound have at least a small claim to their niche among the healing herbs. Horehound is now made into lozenges with honey to soothe sore throats, but it was once considered a cure for the bites of serpents and mad dogs, and an antidote to poisons. Walahfrid Strabo says: "If ever a vicious stepmother mixes in your drink subtle poisons, or makes a treacherous dish of lethal aconite for you, don't waste a moment, take a dose of wholesome horehound."

Lavender's name comes from the Latin *lavare* (to wash), because it took the place of bath salts for the Romans. It is one

of the few herbs whose flowers are more valuable than their leaves or roots; and though the whole plant has a fine aromatic smell, only the flowers and flower stalks produce the essential oil that is used in perfume. They have always been used as we use them today—to scent linens and soaps and perfumes—but at one time they were also kept in bowls in sickrooms or burned there as a disinfectant; and they were an ingredient in the Vinegar of the Four Thieves. Their effect was not entirely imaginary, because the plant contains the disinfectant chemical eucalyptol. In medicine, lavender was valued as a cure for nervous headache—in fact, for "all griefes and paines of the head and brain," and Turner wrote: "Flowers of lavender quilted in a cappe and dayly worn, comfort the braine very well." So it also had its place in the long list of farfetched cures. A preparation that first appeared in the London *Pharmacopoeia* at the end of the seventeenth century contained nearly thirty ingredients, including lavender, sage, rosemary, betony, cowslip, etc., distilled in French brandy. Then spices were added, such as cinnamon, nutmeg, and mace, and the mixture was perfumed and colored with saffron, musk, and red roses. It must have been a pleasant medicine, but we can hardly believe that it was effective against fourteen ailments, from falling-sickness (epilepsy) to barrenness in women.

As the centuries passed, herbal mixtures became more and more complicated, till they very often contained twenty or thirty ingredients. Some herbs were put into electuaries, which were powders mixed with honey or syrup, and part of the powder was often pulverized gems—pearls, emeralds, ivory. Recipes in stillroom books are particularly interesting. One English family that seemed much troubled with "fitts" had five recipes for that affliction, all containing poppies. Mrs. Skillens' recipe for yellow jaundice called for nine earthworms split and cleaned, with a "handfull of Sallendine" and a pennyworth of saffron in ale.

Though those earthworms are hard to understand, saffron and celandine are not, if one is familiar with the Doctrine of Signatures, very popular during the sixteenth and seventeenth centuries. As the herbalist William Coles defined it: "The mercy of God...maketh...Herbes for the use of men, and hath not only stamped upon them a distinct forme, but also given them particular Signatures, whereby a man may read...the use of them." Thus the yellow juice of celandine and the orange stigmas of the saffron crocus were specifics for yellow jaundice; maidenhair fern cured baldness; the daisy (or day's eye) helped sore eyes; plants with hollow stems were good for ailments of the windpipe or the blood vessels. This doctrine was explained and illustrated in many books, and for several centuries it was accepted almost everywhere, even by intelligent people. They found it very comforting to believe that God had carefully provided an herb to protect each part of the human body against every disorder that could possibly attack it, and then had clearly marked the herbs so that no mistakes could be made in using them.

Mistakes were made, as we have seen. Nevertheless, many herbs were—and remain to this day—powerful and efficient healing agents, and hundreds of others have over the ages brought comforting relief from symptoms. As William Coles said, "Most of [these uses] I am confident are true, and if there be any that are not so, yet they are pleasant."

PLANTS BEARING A LIKENESS TO TEETH
Porta: *Phytognomonica*,
Naples, 1588

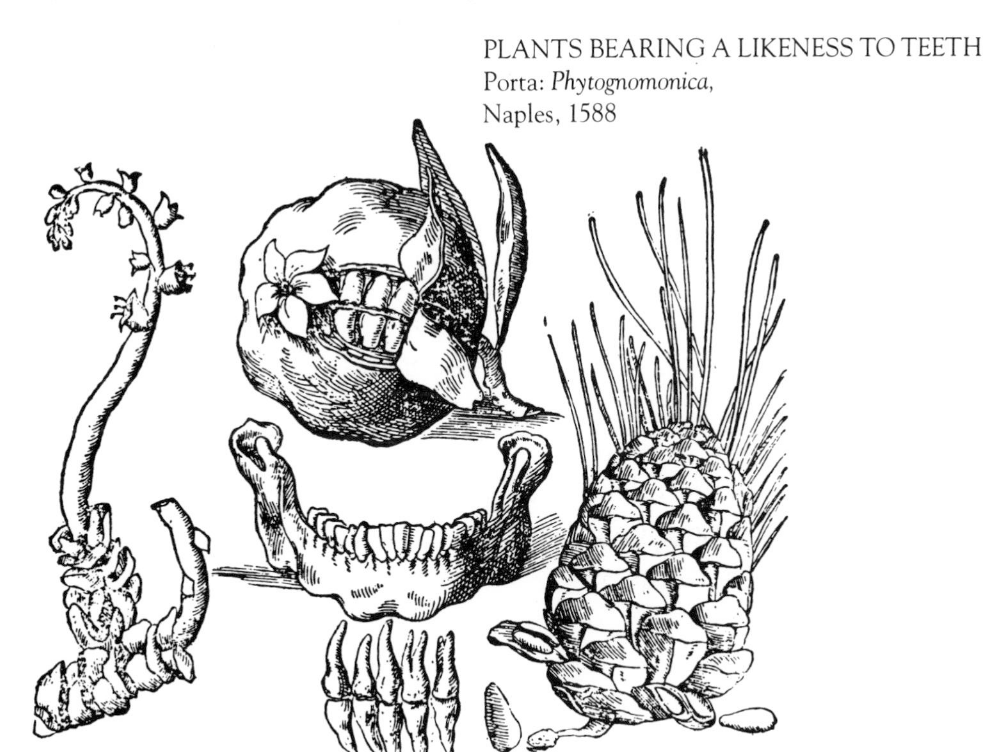

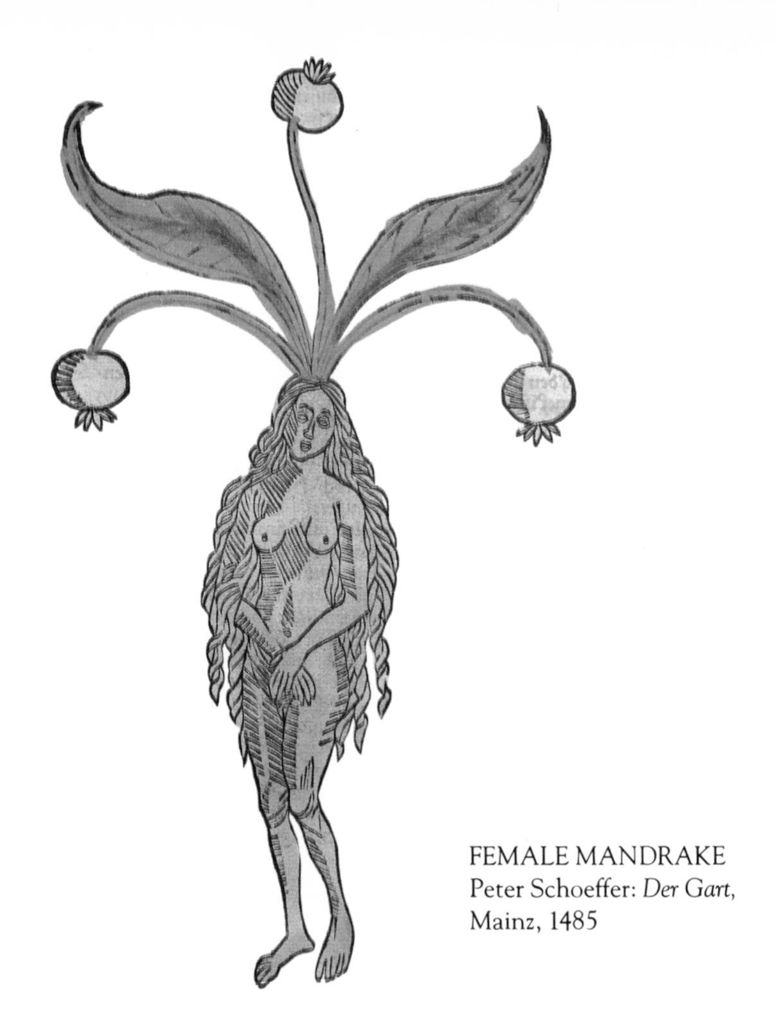

FEMALE MANDRAKE
Peter Schoeffer: *Der Gart*,
Mainz, 1485

ENCHANTED HERBS

If the powers of darkness could make a person sick, they could also interfere with his life in countless other ways. Each day men and women came face to face with dangers they felt powerless to combat alone, so they turned hopefully to magic. Terrified or sick, in love or out of it, but always in trouble, they looked to plants for help with all the problems that so constantly beset them.

Primitive "savages" were not the only ones who relied on magic. Throughout history and around the world, from the bed chamber to the battlefield, it influenced and sometimes gov-

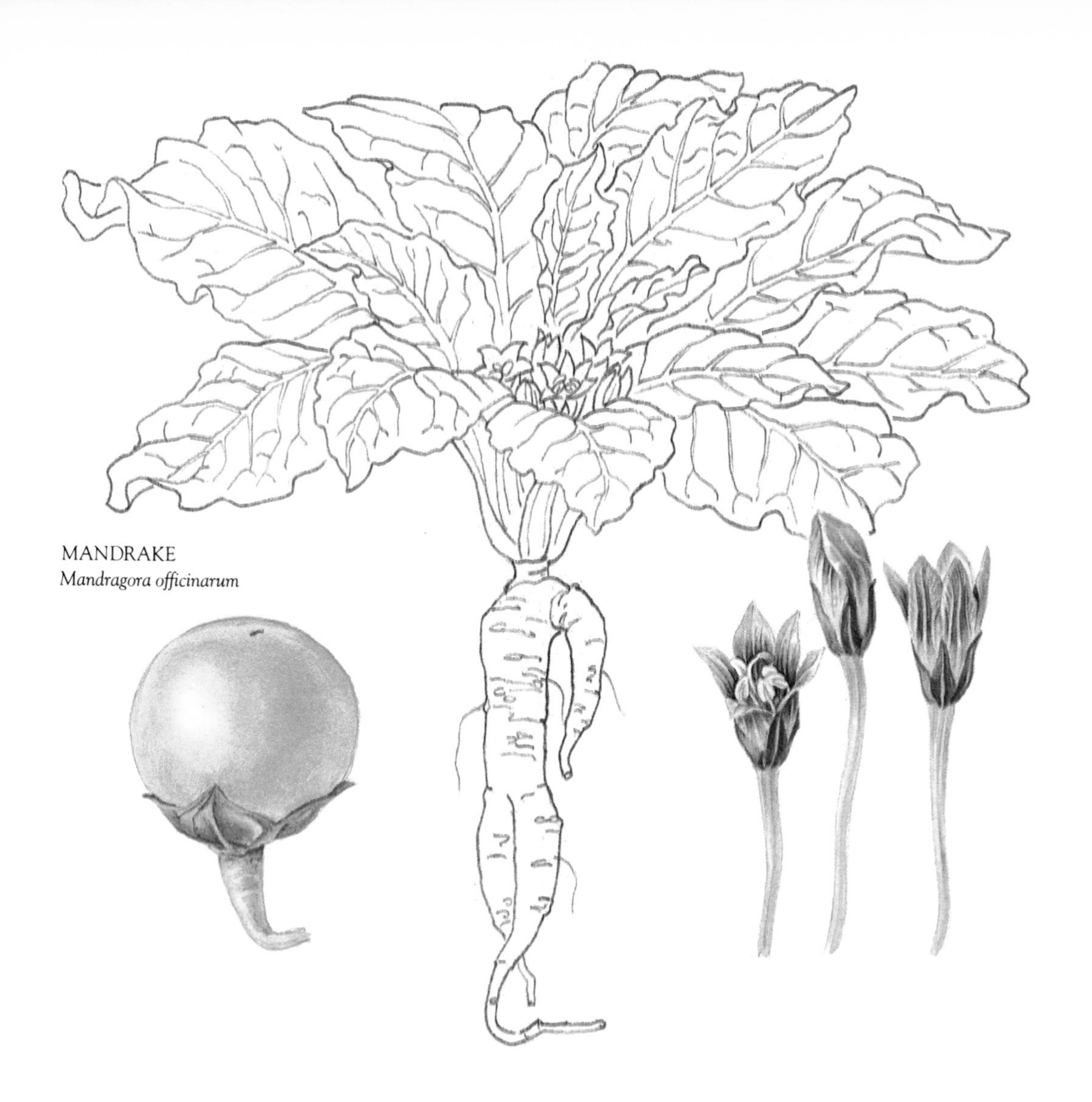
MANDRAKE
Mandragora officinarum

erned people's lives, and the folklore of every country is still interwoven with a complicated magic of herbs. As a result of all this, some plants have been valued more for powers they do not possess than for powers they really have.

One of these is the most fascinating plant in the history of herbs—probably the most fascinating plant in any history—the mandrake. It is a relative of belladonna and henbane, with similar chemical properties, which act on the central nervous system. But long before anything was known about chemistry, it was one of the most sought-after plants in the world. Its tapering roots are shaped rather like those of a carrot, but they often fork in such a way as to look like a human figure. In medieval manuscripts—even scientific ones—mandrake is nearly always pictured as a man or woman with a tuft of leaves for a head, and this human resemblance probably accounts for most of the magical properties it was supposed to have.

The Book of Genesis tells us that Jacob's wife, Leah, conceived a child after she was given some mandrakes found in the fields; and almost to the present day, the mandrake has been considered an herb of supreme power. People went to such fantastic lengths to own a root that there was often a lively trade in fakes. Ownership, however, would seem to be a somewhat mixed blessing if this old account is to be credited: "The devil had a special watch upon this root and unless one succeeded in selling one for less than he gave for it, it would stay about him till his death. Throw it into the fire, into the river or smash it, lose it in the woods, so soon as you reached home, there would be the Mandrake, creeping over the floor, smirking, human fashion, from a shelf or ensconced in your bed." But if you treated it well—bathed it every Friday in wine and clothed it in a new silk dress every month—a mandrake in the house ended all want. If you neglected it, it howled.

Gathering a mandrake was very dangerous, because the root wailed when it was pulled from the earth, and its human shriek brought death to anyone who heard it. A collector knew that he should dig it only on a Friday morning before sunrise, with his ears stopped up with cotton or wax. Or, better still, a dog could be tied to the plant and made to pull it out, so that "it was the dog who died."

Mandrake served so many purposes that one writer claimed "it cures every infirmity—except only death, where there is no help." It was used as an anesthetic in surgery; a narcotic for convulsions and insanity; an aphrodisiac to inspire love and produce children; a renewer of youth; a cure for almost every kind of disease; and as a magical object to exorcise demons, bring good fortune, and foretell the future.

Though mandrake is native in the Mediterranean region, it was carried, with its legends, all over Europe. Eventually the legends spread to China and were attached, almost intact, to another root with a human shape—the ginseng—which the Chinese then used in great quantities. When their native species was nearly extinct, they began to import American ginseng, until it too has become rare in our woods; and since the demand is still great, it now has to be filled mostly by commercial growers. Unlike mandrake, ginseng appears to have little real medical value, though it may possibly be a nerve stimulant that can delay fatigue.

Illness and injury were not the only problems that herbs were expected to relieve. People thought that lightning, fire, and witches could be kept away by houseleeks growing on the roof, and Charlemagne ordered that there should be some on every house. (In America, houseleeks are usually called hen-and-chickens.) The constant threat of ill-willed spirits was combatted with plants like mistletoe, periwinkle, vervain, and pimpernel, carried in the pocket or hung in household garlands; and in some places, cattle were crowned with ivy when first driven out to pasture in the spring.

If there was any season of the year when all supernatural beings, both good and evil, were especially active, it was on Midsummer Eve and Midsummer Day, June 22. This is the time of the summer solstice, when, in some parts of the world, the sun does not set for three days; and it is also the time of the feast of St. John. All magic was doubly powerful then, and Midsummer Eve was by far the best time for gathering, with

GREATER CELANDIN[E]
Chelidonium majus

PERIWINKLE
Vinca minor

great ceremony, many of the plants used by sorcerers to concoct their spells and by ordinary mortals to nullify them. Quite naturally, a very important plant was the one dedicated to the saint himself—St. John's wort. It was hated by every evil spirit, and all over Europe it was carried as a charm or hung in windows so that no demon could enter. Hung in a bedchamber, it would bring dreams of a future husband. It also, of course, was used in medicine, and the Doctrine of Signatures ruled that its reddish juice would heal deep wounds.

For an "amorous medicine," or love philter, periwinkle was important. Known in France as "sorcerer's violet," it also promoted happiness; and its leaves, eaten or worn, had great power against evil spirits, snakes, and spite. In Italy, because it was a symbol of immortality, it was placed in garlands on the coffins of dead children.

St. John's wort was not only a charm against evil; it was a universal balm, sometimes called tout-sain *(all health) in French, or tut-san in English. Periwinkle was used as an astringent and tonic. Ground up with earthworms, it "induceth love between man and wife if it bee used in their meales." Celandine was a drug plant in the Middle Ages, and, added to white wine, it made a lotion to "remove freckles of the visage."*

ST. JOHN'S WORT
Hypericum perforatum

Aristotle first recorded the belief that swallows used greater celandine to restore sight to their young if they were blinded. The plant is therefore sometimes called swallow-wort, and its scientific name comes from the Greek word for swallow. Inevitably, it was considered a cure for various eye troubles, as well as for yellow diseases like jaundice. To this day, its yellow juice is one of the many remedies proposed for warts—as effective as any, because warts have the obliging property of going away by themselves.

Evil spirits have always been much more numerous than good ones. Since people generally looked on the forces of nature with misunderstanding and fear, the supernatural beings they associated with those forces seemed sinister, or at least mischievious, rather than benign. Even elves and fairies—gigantic and fearsome in Anglo-Saxon times—were in

Shakespeare's day capricious and troublesome. The most attractive ones were not averse to playing tricks on human beings.

These later elves and fairies are all associated with plants, mostly hiding in them or sleeping in them, as Shakespeare's Ariel did. But the fairy king, Oberon, in *Midsummer Night's Dream,* used the juice of pansies to make his wife fall in love with a donkey, and then, relenting, cancelled the spell with wormwood. Cowslips, foxgloves, and four-leaf clovers were elfin favorites, and clover was one of the few plants that enabled its wearer to look safely at fairies. Fern seed was worn to make the wearer invisible. (Fern has no seed, but people thought that the seed was merely invisible and could impart that quality to those who carried it.)

Witches used herbs much more than fairies did, in both black magic and white. Their white magic was often borrowed by the village herb women, who knew the medical virtues of wild plants and garden simples, but who usually received their greatest income from the sale of love potions and spells to reveal the future. Among the hundreds of herbs they put into philters, the most used were cyclamen, periwinkle, plantain, and mandrake. They also had plants that could help a love-sick maiden in other ways—celandine would remove her freckles, euphrasia would make her eyes bright, and tansy soaked in buttermilk was good for her complexion. She could gather yarrow from a man's grave and, if she repeated a charm while she placed a sprig under her pillow, it would bring dreams of a husband.

Black magic, on the other hand, was a very serious matter—the province of the Devil himself and of the witches who served him, especially their three queens, Hecate, Medea, and Circe. Their special herbs were the extremely poisonous ones

WITCHES BREWING A STORM
Molitor: *De Lamiis*, 1489

— mandrake, belladonna, hemp, wolfsbane, hemlock, and henbane—but many other plants found their way into brews, since witches could make even harmless plants deadly. These herbs were most effective if "digged in the dark," and they were combined in groups, usually of seven or nine, often with the addition of toads or bats or serpents.

Poison hemlock is a true witches' herb. Every part of the plant contains the very poisonous alkaloid coniine, and Gerard called it "evill, dangerous, hurtfull." Used for centuries as a sedative and antispasmodic, hemlock was a legitimate medicine until very recently; but it is most often thought of as a

POISON HEMLOCK
Conium maculatum

killer. It was the poisonous drink that executioners gave to the Greek philosopher Socrates when he was condemned to death for corrupting the minds of the young; and other ancient philosophers who wanted to commit suicide crowned themselves with garlands and drank hemlock. Throughout Europe, it was a plant of ill omen, a funereal and satanic herb.

Hemlock, along with eye of newt, toe of frog, lizard's leg, and gall of goat, simmered in the cauldron of the three witches who met Macbeth on a wild heath and foretold his bloody future. Prophecy was perhaps the most important occupation of all sorcerers, but sorcerers and demons of any sort were also capable of casting spells on things and people. They could sink

Poison hemlock is a tall, beautiful member of the Carrot family, quite unrelated to the American tree called hemlock. A virulent poison, it kills by paralyzing the motor nerves, leaving the mind unaffected to the end. Mugwort is so called because it was formerly used to flavor beer. Like its close relative wormwood, it is strongly aromatic, and both herbs were folded among woolens to repel moths and fleas.

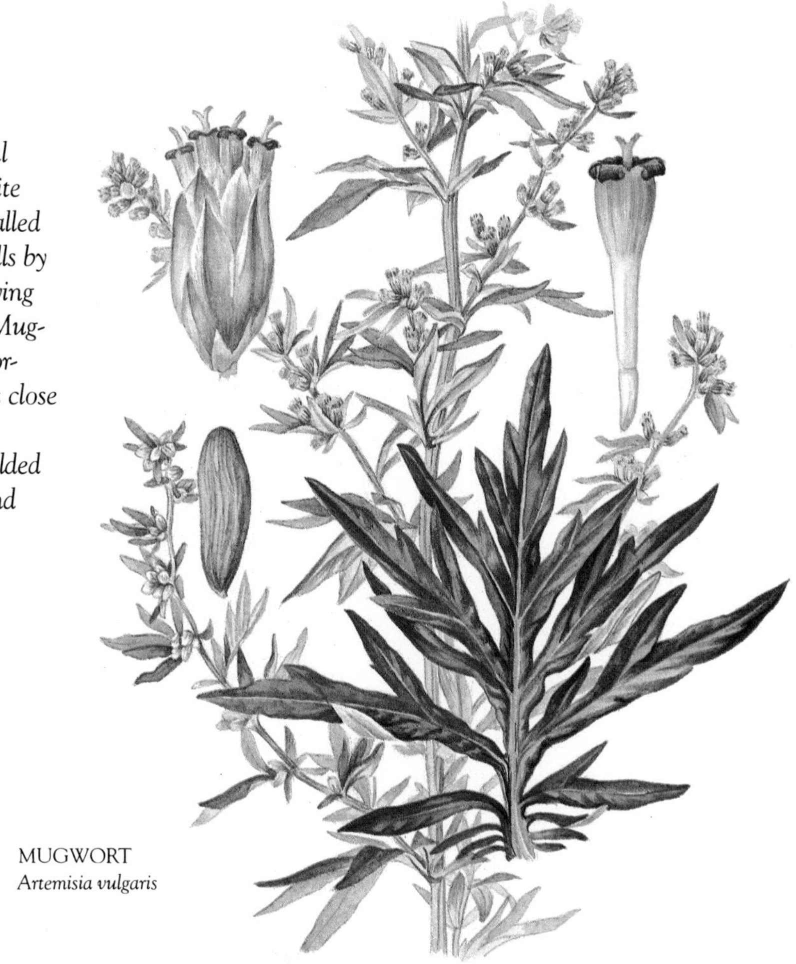

MUGWORT
Artemisia vulgaris

a man's ship or make him waste mysteriously away; his cows might cease to give milk, or his fruit might wither on the tree. Therefore it behooved every individual to be constantly vigilant and to protect himself in all possible ways. Fortunately a great many herbs gave protection, among them St. John's wort, mullein, vervain, dill, and mugwort. Mugwort was one of the Saxons' nine sacred plants. Gathered on Midsummer Eve and worn as a crown or hung in the house, it had great power against weariness, poisons, and devils.

Therefore, with plants like these at hand and with life so hazardous and difficult, a garden of herbs was one kind of insurance no wise person could do without.

THE GRACE THAT LIES IN HERBS

Every spring, with the return of green leaves, we see life emerging from death all around us. Primitive people were even more aware of this resurrection than we are, and the yearly miracle filled them with wonder and awe. If plants were not gods themselves, they thought, they must be inhabited by or controlled by supernatural beings, and fallible men and women must approach them with reverence. Even today, when many of us no longer live close to nature, plants still exercise a real power over our minds and bodies. And they are still woven into the ceremonies and symbolism of nearly all the world's religions.

In prehistoric times, the properties of herbs were secrets learned by the most intelligent and observant individuals, who then became the magicians, medicine men, and priests. Especially secret were the plants that caused stupor or delirium, because the possessors of such secrets could produce trances and other manifestations that could be laid to supernatural causes. The ravings of oracles and the ecstatic visions of many religious groups were induced by such narcotic plants as poppy, hemp (marijuana), and—in the western hemisphere—by the cactus peyote and various mushrooms. In fact, all our present-day narcotics have been linked at some time with religion or magic. They became a social problem only when they moved outside the temple or the pharmacy.

One of the most ancient religious customs is the use of incense. Most incense came from Oriental trees and not from herbs, but occasionally churches burned rosemary instead, and in France it was called "*incensier.*" The Romans garlanded their household gods with rosemary; and the ancient Hebrews anointed tabernacle, ark, and ceremonial vessels with a sacred oil compounded of sweet-flag root with olive, cinnamon, and myrrh. Some plants were sacred in themselves. Lotus and iris were worshiped in Egypt; and holy basil was venerated as a deity in India—a deity that could sanctify, protect, and lead the way to heaven. Its relative, sweet basil, was planted in cemeteries in Persia and scattered on tombs in Egypt.

Plants have been woven into nearly all spiritual rituals—funerals, weddings, sacred games, and festivals—according to the legends and symbolism attached to them. Rosemary, for remembrance, was distributed among the guests at funerals, and sprigs of it were thrown into the grave. In India, after a corpse had been burned, mourners bathed in a nearby river and left on its bank two handfuls of sesame seed as food for the soul of the departed. Fennel was often strewed in the path of bridal couples, and a bride's bouquet usually contained rosemary to insure happiness and a faithful husband. Everybody knows about the laurel wreaths that crowned the victors in many Greek games, but wreaths of parsley were equally common; and at Greek banquets, the guests wore crowns of parsley. Roman banqueters wore many other kinds of plants, especially roses.

Every deity in classical or Norse mythology had his or her special plants. The pink was dedicated to the Roman god Jupiter, the lily and the rose to Juno, the rose and the apple to Venus, the olive to Minerva. Use of these plants was frowned on by the early Christian church; but as the centuries passed, nearly all the ones belonging to important pagan goddesses were gradually accepted and transferred to the Virgin Mary. The rose, the lily, the iris, all became Mary's flowers; and many others, like lady's-mantle and lady's-smock, bore her name because of some symbolic association. Our Lady's bedstraw for instance, was, according to legend, one of the plants on which

Tansy was used in folk medicine for many ills, from wounds to worms to the plague. Its young leaves were beaten with eggs and fried into Easter cakes to counteract the salt-fish diet of Lent, and its bitter flavor was sometimes added to puddings. All this seems rather unwise, because tansy can be toxic. It was better used as a strewing herb to keep out fleas.

TANSY
Tanacetum vulgare

the Christ Child lay in the manger at Bethlehem.

As Christianity spread over Europe, there came to be a plant for nearly every saint in the calendar and a saint for every plant, matched up by date of bloom or some symbolic attribute. St. Francis, who loved all plants and animals, wrote in his "Song of Brother Sun:"

> Praise to you, my Lord, for our sister, Mother Earth,
> Who sustains us, and directs us,
> Gives us different fruits, and colored flowers, and herbs.

Rosemary's Latin name means "dew of the sea." Much valued from ancient times to the present, it decorated the boar's head at Christmas feasts and scented the water for washing hands after meals. It was, and still is, used widely in cooking, and at one time it was important in medicine. Rosemary was reputed to strengthen the memory and to make people "lusty, lively, joyful, liking, and youngly."

ROSEMARY
Rosmarinus officinalis

GOOD HUSWIVES DELIGHT

If the green world subtly influenced all the fears and aspirations of the human mind, it governed the human body with absolute power. Our ancestors quite literally could not have lived without plants. Their dwellings were built wholly or partly from the wood of trees; their garments were woven from plant fibers or from the wool of animals that owed existence to plants; and they ate the leaves, roots, and fruits of plants, or the flesh of animals that ate plants. Directly or indirectly, plants kept people alive and also furnished the materials and tools necessary for everyday housekeeping.

FRAGRANT HERBS
IN THE HOUSE
Petrarch: *Von der Artzney Bayder Glück*, Augsburg, 1532

The homely tasks that have to be performed in every household, from the laundry room to the boudoir, from the great hall to the barnyard, were as unavoidable in the past as they are now, though they were often performed in very different ways. Today, when even the most isolated country people have electric refrigerators, kitchen utensils of plastic, and clothes woven from synthetic fibers, it is hard for us to imagine what it would be like to keep house without such simple "necessities" as steel wool or mothballs or cleaning fluid. And how could we make ourselves beautiful without a place to buy hair dye or cleansing cream?

Life in early Europe was not as romantic as it sometimes appears, and we would have found it generally far from pleasant. When the Roman Empire fell, it took with it all its civilized good living and its municipal services like street lights and running water. After barbarian hordes swept across Europe, many centuries passed before domestic life became pleasant again. A feudal castle about the year A.D. 1000 was not much more comfortable than a peasant's hut—in fact, it might be less comfortable, with its big draughty halls and stone floors and walls. Everything that its occupants wore or ate or used was grown or made at home by hand. Gradually, however, towns and cities were reestablished, traders brought products from distant places, and the quality of life improved. By the late sixteenth century—the Elizabethan Age in England—noblemen and wealthy townspeople lived in luxury again.

Portraits of Henry VIII and Elizabeth I, and paintings of events in their castles and country houses, show us lavish costumes of silk and velvet, embroidered with jewels and trimmed with lace. Household furniture was heavy, but rich with pillows and tapestries, and there were utensils of gold and pewter and glass. It all looks beautiful, but the paintings do not tell us how it smelled. Erasmus deplored the stench he met in English houses, where food thrown to dogs at meals often lay on the floor till it decayed. Table manners were not refined, and those immense velvet skirts must have carried many spots in an age when there was no dry cleaning.

Fresh air was feared and sanitation was unknown, and if it had not been for fragrant herbs, life would scarcely have been tolerable. Gerard tells us that woodruff "being made up into garlands or bundles and hanged up in houses in the heat of Sommer, doth very wel attemper the aire, coole and make fresh the place, to the delight and comfort of such as are therein." Furniture was rubbed with herbs for scent as well as for good luck, and sweet-smelling plants were scattered over the uncar-

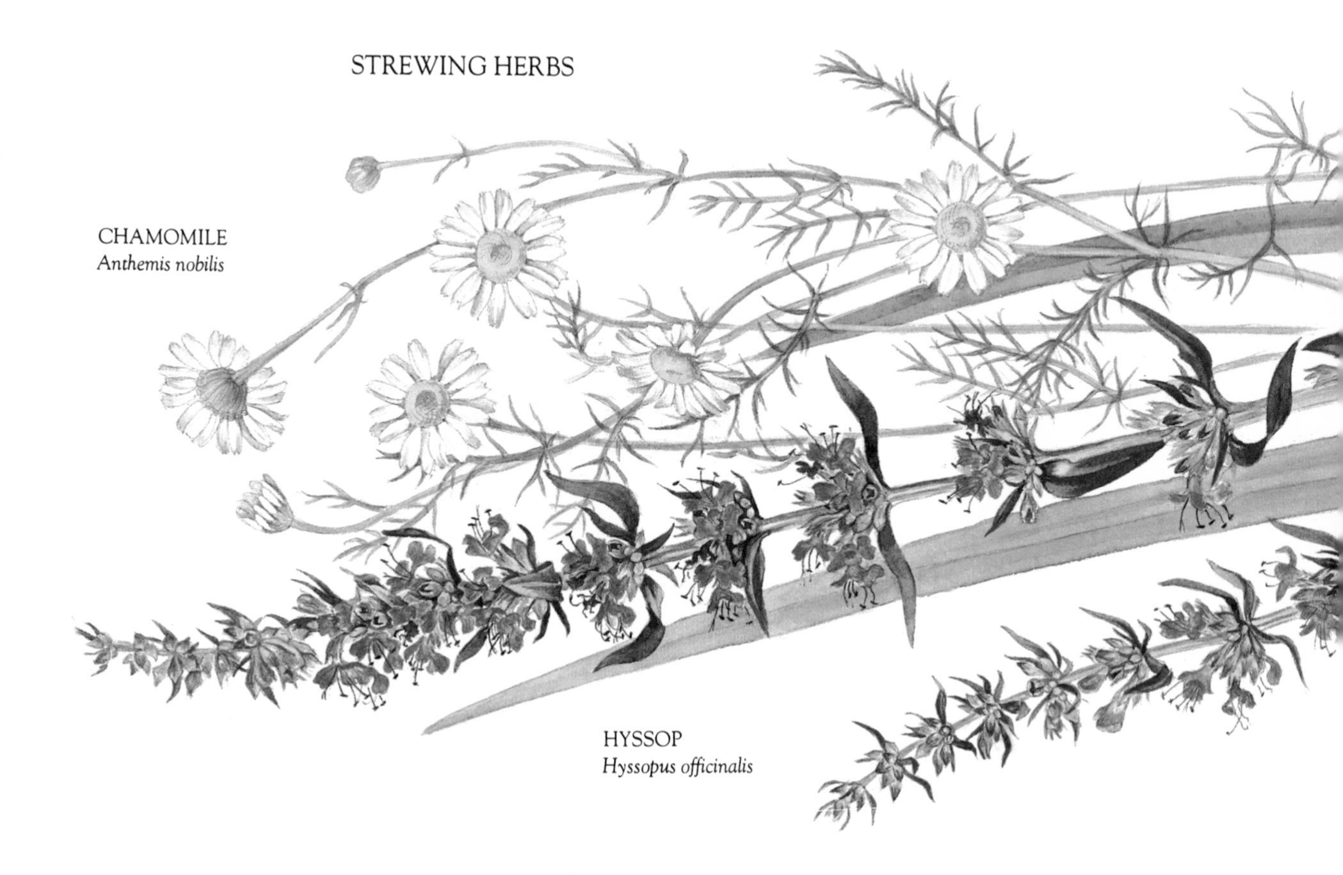

peted floors of cottage, castle, and church. (The kings of England employed a Royal Herb Strewer—an office that was continued at coronations as late as that of George IV in 1820.) Nearly all the aromatic cooking herbs were at times strewed on floors, but tough plants like filipendula, sweet flag, woodruff, lavender, and hyssop were equally fragrant and more durable when walked on.

Sweet flag belongs to the Aram family, but its leaves look very much like those of iris, or flag; and since both plants grow in wet places, they are sometimes hard to tell apart. The leaves and roots of sweet flag have a strong, distinctive fragrance, and

SWEET WOODRUFF
Asperula odorata

SWEET FLAG
Acorus calamus

from Biblical times on, they were used in medicine and perfume. Woodruff, especially when dried, smells like new-mown hay — a delightful perfume for linens, snuff, and potpourri. Chamomile, with a scent like apples, can be grown as a fragrant lawn. It is one of the oldest herbal favorites, dedicated to the gods by the Egyptians and used ever since in many ways — in medicinal baths, in water for washing hands, or as a rinse for blond hair. In Roman days, hyssop was a holy herb, important in purification ceremonies in temples. Monks grew it in their physick gardens and added its bitter taste to pickles, soups, and stuffings.

For a bridal chamber, one would choose strewing herbs that contributed not only their fragrance but also their magic to the marriage—verbena, marjoram, meadowsweet, mint, thyme, valerian, and violet (all sacred to Venus) and basil and broom (sacred to Mars). Or a jar containing these same herbs could be placed on a table, to be stirred occasionally with the fourth finger of the left hand.

Such a mixture of dried herbs is called a potpourri, and there are innumerable recipes in stillroom books for blends of many kinds. Best known are the rose mixtures, which are still made today, even though it is now hard to find the old-fashioned roses whose petals produce and retain scent much better than the petals of modern teas and floribundas. Sometimes these herbal mixtures were burned or boiled so that their smoke or steam filled the house with "comfort." To make King Edward VI's Perfume, one is directed to "take twelve spoonfuls of right red rose water, the weight of sixpence in fine powder of sugar, and boyle it on hot Embers and coals softly and the house will smell as though it were full of Roses, but you must burn the Sweet Cypress wood before to take away the gross ayres."

The smoke of burning herbs was commonly used not only to dispel "gross ayres" but also to fumigate sick rooms and keep the air of houses pure in time of epidemics. Juniper, rosemary, lavender, and bay leaves were most used, and since they all contain antiseptic chemicals like eucalyptol, they may have had more than a psychological effect. Bouquets of these herbs were placed on judges' benches and in the prisoner's dock, and "anti-pestilential" rue was twined around the judge's chair, to preserve him from jail fever and the smell of the prisoners. This custom is still commemorated in England. As late as 1966, at the ceremonial openings of the Assizes at London's Old Bailey prison, every judge and city father was given a bouquet.

Even on the streets, smells and the threat of infection impelled people to carry small bunches of fragrant herbs to hold to their noses while passing through crowds. Among the wealthy, these nosegays, or tussie-mussies, were often replaced by pomanders — small balls of perfume enclosed in jeweled cases. They were made of earth or fine white wax, scented usually with expensive Oriental spices like labdanum and spikenard, fixed with ambergris, civet, or musk. Sometimes they were made even more costly by the addition of powdered gold or gems. The cases, also called pomanders, were designed as beautiful pieces of jewelry to be worn on a chain at the waist or around the neck. They were a favorite New Year's gift (Henry VIII gave one to his daughter Mary) and were handed down as family heirlooms.

The pomander was originally an orange stuffed with spices. Cardinal Wolsey carried one in which the pulp had been replaced by a sponge wet with vinegar and "other confections" and which he "smelt unto" whenever he went into a crowded room. Later, in the seventeenth century, sponges soaked in vinegar were enclosed in pomander cases or in the hollow heads of canes.

Anything that could be washed with soap and water was kept clean, though the soaps of those days would seem inadequate to a modern housewife. They were often made from the alkali of burned bracken fern or from soapwort, which we call bouncing Bet. Once washed, the elaborate linen ruffs worn by Elizabethan men and women had to be stiffened with perfumed starch and shaped on "poking sticks." This starch usually came from the bulbs of English bluebells, or scillas, which Gerard says, made "the best starch next unto that of Wake-robin roots" (a kind of jack-in-the-pulpit). Long before that—in about A.D. 850—orris, the powdered root of Florentine iris, was used to

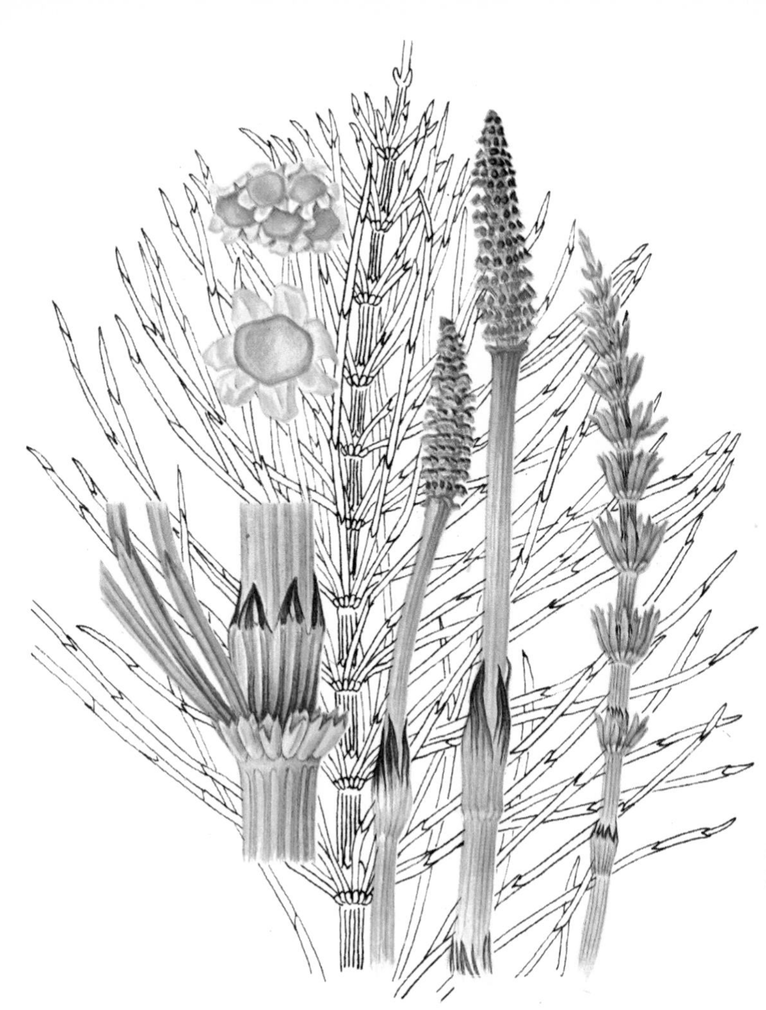

Scouring rush was often called pewterwort. In addition to polishing metal, it served in medicine, chiefly as an astringent. Pyrethrum and monkshood are both common in today's flower gardens. Pyrethrum is usually called "painted daisy," and monkshood often goes by its scientific name, aconite. Legend says that monkshood was created by the witch Hecate from the frothing saliva of Cerberus, the dog that guarded the gate to Hell.

SCOURING RUSH
Equisetum arvense

"stiffen shining linen and scent it sweetly;" and in the eighteenth century, the same powder stiffened and whitened the enormous wigs the ladies wore. It is now used to perfume face powder and other cosmetics.

In the household, from the scullery to the library, there were few tasks that did not involve herbs. Brushes were made from Scotch broom and butcher's broom, pens and rushlights from reeds, paste from scilla bulbs. Pots and pans and pewter plates, and even knightly armor, were polished with scouring rushes—our common horsetails. Silica deposits in the stems of these plants make them both rough and tough; and a Dutch species, with an especially large amount of silica, was very popular in

England. This forerunner of steel wool was efficient enough to be used by cabinetmakers and arrowsmiths, and it can still serve very well for scouring aluminum.

Good housewives have always folded lavender, rosemary, and southernwood among their woolens to protect them from moths, and at one time pennyroyal was scattered among the strewing herbs to deter fleas, while tansy was used to discourage ants. More serious pests, from head lice to rats to wolves, were exterminated with the truly virulent poisons—aconite, hellebore, larkspur, and pyrethrum. Pyrethrum flowers are the source of its poison, which kills insects without harming warm-blooded animals. It is still an effective and safe garden spray and is now produced commercially.

Aconite, or monkshood, or wolfsbane, was long considered the deadliest of all poisons. From all parts of the plant, but especially from its roots, come alkaloids that have a powerful depressant effect on the heart, and the plant was until recently an official drug. In ancient times, it was used by invading armies to poison wells, as an arrow poison for lion hunters in India, and as wolf and rat bait in Europe. It was also part of the stock-in-trade of all people-poisoners, from the court of Augustus Caesar to that of the Borgias. Livy wrote that kings always kept poisons on hand "for the uncertainties of fate," and many people besides kings have resorted to aconite to do away with their enemies or themselves. It was the herb that Medea prepared for Theseus and the one that Romeo swallowed in his grief when he thought that Juliet was dead.

The earliest dyes nearly all came from plants. At first, primitive people simply smeared berry juice on their weapons, their utensils, or their bodies. But by 3000 B.C. the true craft of dyeing cloth was known in China; and in India about 2500 B.C. fabrics were colored with a red purple from the madder plant and a blue from indigo. Egyptian mummy wrappings from about 2000 B.C. were dyed blue with either indigo or woad; and at nearly the same time, the Egyptians were using safflower for yellows and reds. Pliny writes of the dye recipes of his day and mentions skilled dyers in Gaul who used vegetable pigments. All the life and color of the Middle Ages came from plant dyes, which tinted the wools of the intricately pictured tapestries as well as the bright fabrics of clothing and tournament banners.

Every part of the world has its own dye plants. In Europe, about two dozen were found to be efficient enough to be used regularly and cultivated. Some of the most important, in addition to madder, were dyer's woad, which gives a blue dye;

REMOVING HEAD LICE
Hortus Sanitatis,
Mainz, 1491

genista, which gives a yellow; alkanet, a red; bedstraw, reds and yellows; and saffron, a yellow.

Saffron yellow and Tyrian purple are perhaps the most famous colors in literature and history. The purple was made from a kind of seashell, but the saffron came from the stigmas of the same crocus that was once important in medicine and is still important in cooking. Mentioned in the Bible, treasured by the Greeks and Romans, extravagantly admired in the Orient, it has been a luxury item for at least four thousand years. Because 60,000 crocus flowers produce only one pound of saffron, it was always expensive, but in England (and other places as well), enormous amounts were used. In the time of Henry VIII, court ladies dyed their hair with saffron and used so much of it that the king forbade the practice, fearing that none of his favorite herb would be left to flavor his food. Saffron dyed the shoes of Persian kings, and it was sometimes

used in place of gold leaf in the illumination of medieval manuscripts.

The blue color from woad was the most important dye of medieval Europe. The plant that produced it was common throughout western Asia and Europe, and when Caesar first came to Britain, he found that the natives there stained their skins with it. It was widely cultivated; and, since crops were not successful for more than two years in one place, early woad growers led a wandering life. Later, they learned how to rotate their crops.

The red color from alkanet was a face paint from Egyptian times to the seventeenth century, and it is still used occasion-

HERBS FOR DYE

Saffron comes from the long orange stigmas that are part of the pistil of this species of crocus. A precious commodity throughout history, it has been important in religion and medicine, and as a dye, a flavoring, and a perfume. It is still used to flavor food, especially rice. Alkanet's red dye comes from the rind of its root; the blue of woad comes from its leaves; and the yellow of genista is produced by all parts of the plant, but especially the flowers.

SAFFRON CROCUS
Crocus sativus

ally to tint ointment. It also stained wood and marble, but was most important as a dye for cloth. Genista, or dyer's greenweed, gives a yellow dye that was combined with the blue of woad to make green. It was known and used from earliest times, for medicine and seasoning as well as for color. This "genet plant" was the ancient emblem of Brittany, and it gave its name to the royal house of Plantagenet.

All the beautiful vegetable dyes were crowded out in the nineteenth century by the more permanent analine dyes and synthetic colors. Now, however, they are being revived, not in industry, but by artists who value their soft, rich hues for handwoven fabrics, and who are experimenting with colors extracted from a great many new plants in addition to the ancient ones.

For the fabrics themselves, plants also provided fibers—flax, cotton, and hemp—but such plants have always been grown as an agricultural crop and can scarcely be thought of as herbs.

In northern Europe, linen and wool were for centuries the only important fabrics for wardrobe and household. (We still speak of "bed linens" and "table linens.") Trade with the Orient eventually brought in silk and cotton, but sheep raising and the weaving of woolen cloth have always been leading industries there. From the time of the earliest weavers, the teasel plant was used to "tease" or raise the nap of woolen cloth; and its seed heads, with their sharply toothed bracts, have served the same purpose in woolen mills almost to the present day. No metal prongs could be invented that would scratch the cloth lightly without tearing it, but very recently, plastic teasels have been introduced, reproducing almost perfectly the action of the plant heads.

Nearly all these ancient uses of herbs, most of them so pleasant, seem remote to us now—made obsolete by the march of modern industry and science. But we can remember, when we walk in an herb garden and brush a fragrant plant or when we pick a leaf to flavor a salad, that there was a time when an herb garden was not intended to be a pleasure garden and its plants were growing there only for the purest utility.

THE PRAISE OF COOKS

In the kitchen alone, herbs are as important today as they ever were. For a long period, this was not true, and herb cookery, at least in England and America, went into almost total eclipse. Twenty-five years ago, after a slow decline of a century or more, it was merely a fad indulged in by a few enthusiastic gardeners and inspired cooks. This unfortunate state of affairs is now corrected; the virtues of herbs have been rediscovered; and herbs are again making their enormous contributions to our pleasure and well-being. They went into eclipse when they ceased to be a necessity, and they have returned to us as an art.

For centuries, herbs *were* a necessity. It is easy to forget the problems cooks faced in the days when there was no refrigeration and no rapid transportation. Meat could be preserved only by drying, smoking, or salting, and the only vegetables available in winter were the roots and seeds that could be stored. People's diet was limited and monotonous; vitamins were scarce; and meat was nearly always tainted. Eating would have been a dreary business without herbs and spices to cover up unpleasant tastes and give zest to dull menus. In hot countries, where meat spoiled even faster than in the north, it was made palatable by hot spicy sauces — the curries of India and the molés of Mexico.

Long before the time of Christ, people who lived in the countries around the Mediterranean—Egypt, the Holy Land, Greece, and Rome—grew many of the same vegetables we eat today. Among them were cabbages, onions, turnips, beets, lentils, beans, peas, and carrots; and these same plants appear in the vegetable lists of medieval Europe. They were called "potherbs," and most of them had medical as well as gastronomical uses. So also did the "salad herbs" like lettuce, chicory, and cress. Potherbs were much valued in Biblical and Roman times, but in the Middle Ages they were considered food for peasants, to be eaten by the gentry only on fast days. However, no one went hungry in the houses of kings and nobles, where there were always great quantities of meat,

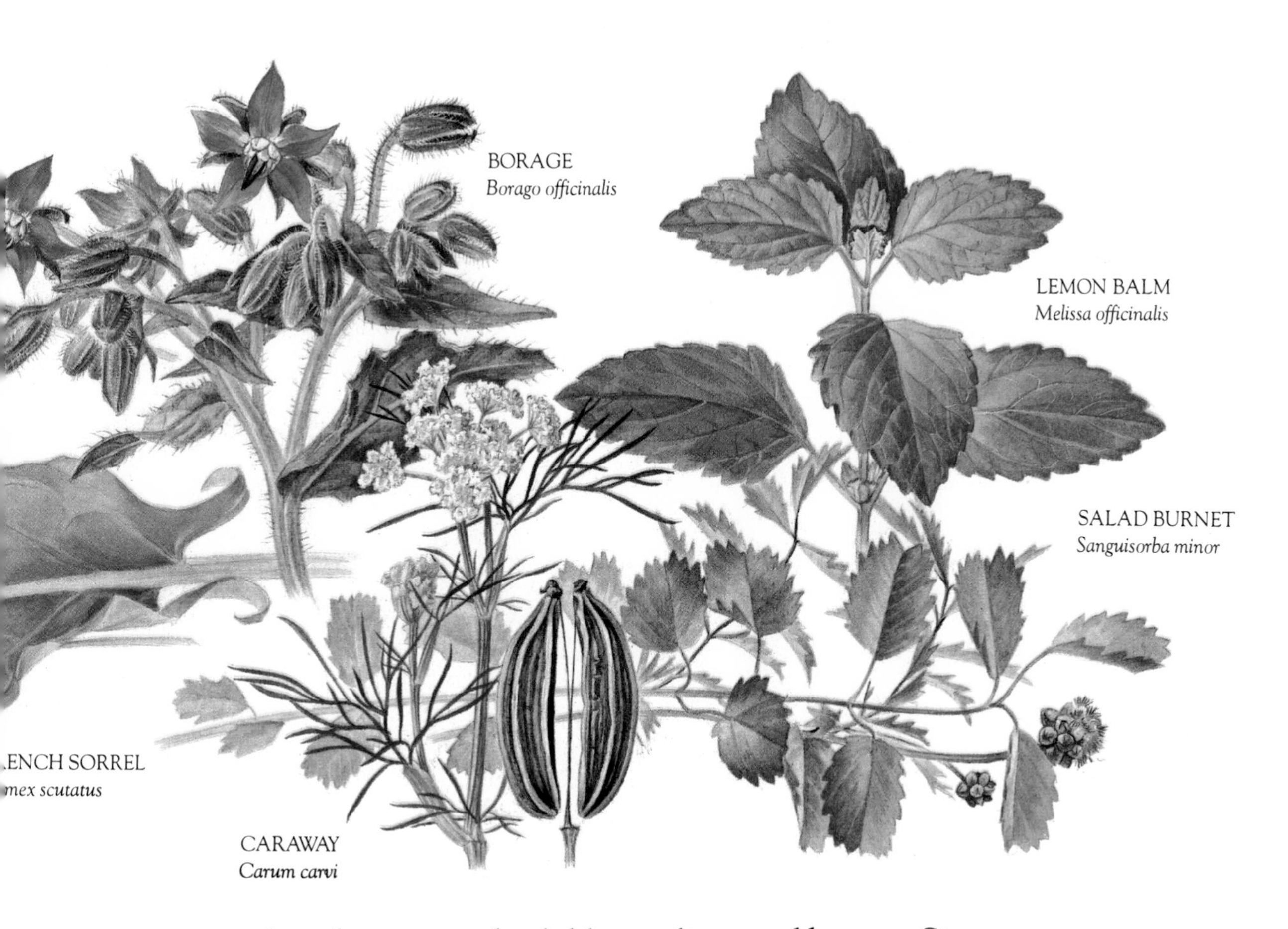

game, and poultry—even birds like starlings and herons. Since the meat and game were only occasionally tender enough to be roasted on a spit, it was most often boiled in elaborate stews or hashes, liberally flavored with herbs and spices, especially pepper, mustard, and garlic. Fruits were popular, but they were preserved in honey or cooked in pastry and seldom eaten raw. It was, in general, a meat-and-pastry diet, not one that a modern nutritionist would recommend.

By the sixteenth century, however, interest in vegetables and salads revived, and people again got their vitamins. Salads especially were important—very complex affairs with as many as thirty ingredients. Their variety was remarkable, with all kinds of greens we would never think of using—strawberry

MEDIEVAL COOKING
Küchenmeisterey,
Augsburg, 1507

leaves, daisy leaves, fresh and candied flowers, elder buds. "Crowned salads" were elaborate castles of vegetables and salad greens, which might well stand as the chief decoration on a banquet table. Vegetables too were served with a flourish, and roots like beet and carrot were cut into fantastic shapes, but even so, vegetables were few as compared with the hundreds of herbs that every cook kept in his larder.

Herbs were, and still are, the chief flavoring ingredients of nearly all liqueurs. As many as a hundred and thirty of them may be added to an alcoholic base like brandy, and their complicated formulas are the secrets of their makers—often monasteries. Wormwood contributes its flavor, and its name, to vermouth; and, with elecampane, it is also an ingredient in absinthe. Saffron and turmeric are often used as colorings.

Nearly all today's kitchen herbs have been in continuous use since the time when garlic was eaten by Egyptian pyramid builders and dill, mint, and rue were paid as tithes in Biblical Israel. They sometimes doubled as medicine, magic, or cosmetic, but in cooking their contribution has remained the same through all those centuries. There are, however, some other plants, once popular, that are no longer used in cooking and are now promoted—or demoted—to the ornamental flower bed.

Roses, for instance, always a source of perfume, were at one time equally important for medicine and food. Roman cooks used them lavishly. Then, after almost disappearing from the medieval kitchen, they became popular again in the seventeenth century; and for two hundred years rose water was used as commonly as we use vanilla today, for the same purposes. There were also rose puddings, rose syrups, and rose conserves, made from both the flower petals and the fruits.

The garden pink, or gillyflower, was such a common flavoring in beer, ale, and wine that in some places it was called "sops-in-wine." It was also pickled, made into conserves and candies, and used to color and flavor a tansie (a sort of sweet omelet).

Marigolds—that is, pot marigolds or calendulas—were a commonplace staple in the European kitchen from Roman times on. Barrels full of the dried, yellow florets were kept on hand because, as Gerard says, "no broths are well made without dried Marigoldes." They seasoned and colored a broth

It was believed that dreaming about marigolds was a happy augury and that looking at the plant drew evil humors out of the head. Its flowers and leaves were used in medicine–among other things, to bring out the rash in measles. Cowslips were as important in medicine as in cooking. They were prescribed for palsy, gout, and other pains in the joints. In white wine, sometimes with cucumbers, they were a face wash that removed freckles and wrinkles and made the complexion "splendent."

MARIGOLD
Calendula officinalis

in which sparrows and larks were stewed; and they also flavored puddings, dumplings, and possets (a kind of drink made with milk and beer). Their yellow florets tinted cheese, were the source of a dye, and sometimes replaced saffron in medicine and cookery.

Cowslips—those flowers beloved of fairies—were also loved by cooks, especially in Elizabethan England. Their young shoots, flowers, and buds were pickled or eaten as salads; and their leaves were cooked as potherbs or added to the stuffing of meats. Cowslip wine, made from the flowers, is still a country drink, and there were also cowslip tansies and cowslip puddings. Every stillroom book had recipes like this one of 1747:

COWSLIP
Primula veris

Cowslip Pudding

Having got the flowers of a peck of Cowslips, cut them small and pound them with half a pound of Naples biscuits grated and three pints of cream. Boil them a little; then take them off the fire, and beat up sixteen eggs, with a little cream and a little rose-water. Sweeten to your palate. Mix it well together, butter a dish and pour it in. Bake and when it is enough, throw fine sugar over and serve it up.

It seems sad that all these interesting and apparently delicious dishes were dropped from the kitchen repertory. But of course, hundreds of other recipes have replaced them—so many recipes in so many fine cookbooks that we will not repeat any of them here. One thing is characteristic of them all: modern cooks use herbs to emphasize the flavor of food, not to mask it; and skilled herbal cooking is an expression of imagination and sophisticated taste. The use of flavorings is a very individual matter, and creative cooks really need no guidelines; but there are a few generally accepted "rules" about what herb goes well with what. These are given here as charts.

Though excellent packaged herbs are available nearly everywhere, using them is never quite the same as gathering the plants fresh from one's own garden. They are at their best when they contain the greatest amount of aromatic oil—just before the flowers are ready to open—and they should be cut on a dry morning after the dew is gone but before the sun is hot. If they are to be kept for later use, herbs can be dried in many ways, but most often they are tied in bunches and hung out of the sun, in a room with even heat. When perfectly dry, they should be stored in tight glass or pottery containers. As long as they are not crushed, their flavor-bearing oils will remain sealed in the plant indefinitely.

Long after they have left the garden, they will still be delicious, ready to flavor a fish sauce, to stuff a chicken, or to "comfort the heart and spirits" in an herb tea. The cook who intends to do any of these things might well remember John Evelyn's 1699 advice about salad making:

> Every plant should bear its part without being overpowered by some Herb of stronger taste, so as to endanger the native Sapor and Vertue of the rest; but fall into places like Notes in Music, in which should be nothing harsh or grating and tho admitting some discords...reconcile all dissonances and melt them into an agreeable composition.

Uses of Herbs in Cooking

WITH BEEF
basil
celery
horseradish
lovage
parsley
rosemary
summer savory
sweet marjoram

WITH LAMB
dill
garlic
mint
rosemary
summer savory
sweet marjoram

WITH PORK
basil
chives
rosemary
sage
summer savory
sweet marjoram
coriander (in sausage)

WITH VEAL
horseradish
rosemary
sage
summer savory
sweet marjoram
thyme

WITH POULTRY
chervil
rosemary
sage
summer savory
sweet marjoram
tarragon
thyme

WITH EGGS
basil
chervil
chives
summer savory
sweet marjoram
tarragon
thyme (continued)

Uses of Herbs in Cooking

WITH FISH

basil
chervil
dill
chives
fennel
parsley
sage
sweet marjoram
tarragon
thyme

FOR TEAS

angelica
anise
bergamot
catnip
chamomile
fennel
horehound
lemon balm
lemon verbena
lovage
pennyroyal
peppermint
rosemary
saffron
sage
spearmint
sweet marjoram
thyme

IN SOUPS

anise
bay leaf
calendula
chervil
chives
cumin
dill
fennel
parsley
thyme

IN BREADS, CAKES, AND COOKIES

anise
caraway
coriander
cumin
fennel
poppy
sesame

IN SWEETS

anise
borage (flowers)
caraway
coriander
lovage
peppermint
sesame

FOR SALADS

basil
borage
burnet
calendula
caraway
celery
chervil
chicory
chives
cress
dill
fennel
lovage
nasturtium
sorrel
summer savory
sweet marjoram
tarragon

Plant Families of Herbs That Appear in This Book

Horsetail family *(Equisetaceae)*
scouring rush

Aram family *(Aracaceae)*
sweet flag

Lily family *(Liliaceae)*
autumn crocus, chives, garlic

Iris family *(Iridaceae)*
Florentine iris, saffron crocus

Carnation family *(Caryophyllaceae)*
pink, soapwort

Buttercup family *(Ranunculaceae)*
monkshood, larkspur

Poppy family *(Papaveraceae)*
greater celandine, opium poppy

Mustard family *(Cruciferae)*
black mustard, white mustard, woad, radish, turnip, cresses

Rose family *(Rosaceae)*
burnet, filipendula, lady's-mantle, rose

Pea family *(Leguminosae)*
genista, indigo, Scotch broom

Geranium family *(Geraniaceae)*
scented geraniums

Rue family *(Rutaceae)*
rue

St. John's wort family *(Hypericaceae)*
St. John's wort

Violet family *(Violaceae)*
sweet violet, pansy

Carrot family *(Umbelliferae)*
angelica, anise, caraway, carrot, celery, chervil, coriander, cumin, dill, fennel, hemlock, lovage, parsley, parsnip

Primrose family *(Primulaceae)*
cowslip, primrose

Dogbane family *(Apocynaceae)*
periwinkle

Borage family *(Boraginaceae)*
alkanet, borage, comfrey

Vervain family *(Verbenaceae)*
lemon verbena, vervain

Mint family *(Labiatae)*
basil, betony, bergamot, catnip, horehound, hyssop, lavender, lemon balm, marjorams, mints, pennyroyal, rosemary, sages, savories, thymes

Nightshade family *(Solanaceae)*
belladonna, henbane, potato, thorn apple, tomato, tobacco

Figwort family *(Scrophulariaceae)*
foxglove

(continued)

Plant Families of Herbs That Appear in This Book

(continued from page 75)

Madder family *(Rubiaceae)*
bedstraws, madder, woodruff

Valerian family *(Valerianaceae)*
valerian

Teasel family *(Dipsacaceae)*
teasel

Daisy family *(Compositae)*
calendula, chamomile, chicory, coltsfoot, costmary, daisy, elecampane, mugwort, pyrethrum, safflower, southernwood, tansy, tarragon, wormwoods, yarrow

Some Old Herbals Available in Reprints

COLES, WILLIAM, *The Art of Simpling.* London, 1656.
Reprint: Clarkson, Milford, Conn., 1938.

CULPEPER, NICHOLAS, *Culpeper's Complete Herbal.* 1653.
Reprints: London, 1847; H. Joseph, London, 1947; W. Foulsham, London, 1952.

GERARD, JOHN, *The Herball.* London, 1633.
Reprint: Dover Publications, New York, 1975.

PARKINSON, JOHN, *Paradisi in Sole.* London, 1629.
Reprint: Methuen and Company, 1914.

TUSSER, THOMAS, *Five Hundred Pointes of Good Husbandrie.* 1573.
Reprints: Country Life Ltd., London, 1931; James Tregaskis and Son, London, 1931.

WALAHFRID STRABO, *Hortulus.* c. 845.
Reprint: Translation by Raef Payne, Hunt Botanical Library, Pittsburgh, 1966.

Some Books About Herbs

CLARKSON, ROSETTA E., *Green Enchantment.* Macmillan Company, New York, 1940.

———*Magic Gardens.* Macmillan Company, New York, 1939.

EDLIN, H. L., *British Plants and Their Uses.* B. T. Batsford Ltd., London, 1951.

FOLKARD, RICHARD, *Plant Lore, Legends, and Lyrics.* Samson Low, Marston, Searle, and Rivington, London, 1884.

FOSTER, GERTRUDE B., *Herbs for Every Garden.* E. P. Dutton and Company, New York, 1966.

FREEMAN, MARGARET B., *Herbs for the Mediaeval Household.* Metropolitan Museum of Art, New York, 1943.

GRIEVE, MRS. MAUDE, *A Modern Herbal.* Harcourt, Brace, and Co., New York, 1931.

GRIGSON, GEOFFREY, *A Herbal of All Sorts.* Macmillan Company, New York, 1959.

HOLLINGSWORTH, BUCKNER, *Flower Chronicles.* Rutgers University Press, New Jersey, 1958.

KREIG, MARGARET, *Green Medicine.* Rand McNally and Company, New York, 1964.

NORTHCOTE, LADY ROSALIND, *The Book of Herbs.* John Lane, London, 1903.

RANSON, FLORENCE, *British Herbs.* Penguin Books, Harmondsworth, Middlesex, 1949.

RHODE, ELEANOUR S., *Shakespeare's Wild Flowers and Fairy Lore.* Medici Society, London, 1963.

INDEX

(Page numbers in italics indicate illustrations.)

aconite, 34, 59, *59*, 60
Aconitum napellus (monkshood), 34, 59, *59*, 60
Acorus calamus (sweet flag), 48, 54-55, *55*
Aesculapius, 21
alchemy, 20, 33
alkanet, 61, 62, *62*, 63
Allium schoenoprasum (chives), *14*
Althaea officinalis (marshmallow), 19, *19*
Anchusa tinctoria (alkanet), 61, 62, *62*, 63
Anethum graveolens (dill), 18, *18*, 47, 69
Anthemis nobilis (chamomile), *54*, 55
Arab physicians, 16-17
Aram family, 54
Aristotle, 16, 42
aromatic herbs, 11, 22, 27, 35-36, 47, 52, 53-54, 56-58, 72
Artemisia, 12
Artemisia abrotanum (southernwood), 59
Artemisia dracunculus (tarragon), *15*
Artemisia vulgaris (mugwort), 47, *47*
Asperula odorata (sweet woodruff), 53-55, *55*
astrology, 33
Atropa belladonna (belladonna), 25-27, *26*, 29, 39, 45
Augustine, Saint, 16
autumn crocus, 24, 36, 61, 63
Aztecs, herbal remedies of, 28

basil, *15*, 49, 56
bay leaf, 56
bedstraw, 61
belladonna, 25-27, *26*, 29, 39, 45
betony, 33-34, 35, *35*, 36
bluebell, English, 57
borage, *67*
Borago officinalis (borage), *67*
botanical knowledge, 9, 11, 15-20
bouncing Bet, 57
bracken fern, 57
Brassica nigra (mustard), 66
broom, 56
bryony, 33
burnet, salad, *67*
butcher's broom, 58

cactus peyote, 48
calendula, 69
Calendula officinalis (marigold), 69-70, *70*, 71
caraway, *67*
Carrot family, 11, 47
Carum carvi (caraway), *67*
celandine, 36, *42*, 43, 44
chamomile, *54*, 55
Charlemagne, 17, 22, 41
Chelidonium majus (greater celandine), 36, *42*, 43, 44
chicory, 12, 66
China, 14, 49, 60
chives, *14*
Christianity, 49-50
Chrysanthemum coccineum (pyrethrum), 59-60, *59*
clover, 22, 44
Colchicum autumnale (autumn crocus), 24, 36, 61, 63
Coles, William, 36, 37
coltsfoot, 12, 21
comfrey, *34*, 35
Composite family, 11
Conium maculatum (poison hemlock), 33, 45-46, *46*, 47
cooking, herbs used in, 18, 63, 65-72
coriander, *15*, 29
Coriandrum sativum (coriander), *15*, 29
cotton, 29, 64
cowslip, 36, 44, 70, 71, *71*
cowslip pudding, recipe for, 71
cress, 66
crocus, 24, 36, 61, 63
Culpeper, Nicholas, 20
cyclamen, 44

Daisy, 36
Dark Ages, 17, 53
Datura stramonium (thorn apple), 25, *26*, 27-28
digitalis, 12, 29
Digitalis purpurea (foxglove), 12, 29, 31, *31*, 44
dill, 18, *18*, 47, 69
Dioscorides, 16, 17, 19
Doctrine of Signatures, 36-37, 42
drugs, 29-33, 48
dyer's woad, 60, 62, *62*, 63
dyes, 60-64

Egyptians, ancient, 14, 15, 35, 49, 55, 60, 66, 69
elecampane, *10*, 12, 22, 69
electuaries, 36
England, Elizabethan, 53, 56-57, 70
Endymion non-scriptus, 57, 58
Equisetum arvense (scouring rush), 58-59, *59*
Erasmus, 53
euphrasia, 44
Evelyn, John, *72*

fairies, 29, 31, 43-45
fennel, *14*, 49
fern, 44
Filipendula, 54
flag, 54
Florentine iris, 57
food and drug laws, 32
Foeniculum officinalis (fennel), *14*, 49

four-leaf clover, 44
foxglove, 12, 29, 31, *31,* 44
Francis, Saint, 50
French sorrel, *67*

garden pink, 69
genista, 61, 62, 63
Genista tinctoria (genista), 61, *62,* 63
Gerard, John, 20, 23, 26, 29, 31, 45, 53, 57, 69
ginseng, 41
greater celandine, *42*
Greeks, ancient, 16, 17, 21, 27, 31, 49, 61, 66

head lice, removal of, 59, *61*
Hebrews, ancient, 15, 40, 48-49
hellebore, 59
hemlock, poison, 33, 45-46, *46,* 47
hemp, 45, 48, 64
henbane, 12, 25, 26-27, *27,* 33, 39, 45
Henry VIII (king of England), 57, 61
herbals, 19-20
herb garden, *8,* 12, 64
herbs:
- appearance of, 12
- books about, 76-77
- cooking with, 18, 54, 63, 65-72, *68,* 73-74
- definition of, 9-10
- flowers of, 12
- household uses of, 10, 51-64, *52, 61, 68, 73*
- medical use of, *see* medicine, herbal
- names of, 12, 22, 25, 27, 34, 49-50
- religious symbolism of, 27, 30, 48-50, 56

Hippocrates, 16
holy basil, 49
horehound, 34, 35, *35*
horsetail, 58-59
Hortus Sanitatis, 20, *25*
houseleek, 41
Hyoscyamus niger (henbane), 12, 25, 26-27, *27,* 33, 39, 45
Hypericum perforatum (St. John's wort), 12, 42, 43, *43,* 47, 75
Hyssop, 54, *54,* 55
Hyssopus officinalis (hyssop), 54, *54,* 55

Incas, 28
incense, 48
India, 14, 49, 60, 65
indigo, 60
Inula helenium (elecampane), *10,* 12, 22, 69
iris, 12, 49, 54
Iris germanica var. *florentina* (Florentine iris), 57
Isatis tinctoria (dyer's woad), 60, 62, *62,* 63
ivy, 41

jimsonweed, *see* thorn apple
juniper, 56

lady's-mantle, 49
lady's-smock, 49
larkspur, 59
Lavandula officinalis (lavender), 34-36, *35,* 54, 56, 59
lavender, 34-36, *35,* 54, 56, 59
lemon balm, *67*
lettuce, 66
Levisticum officinale (lovage), *14*
licorice, 29
lily, 49
Lily family, 75
lily of the valley, 24
liqueurs, herbs used in, 68-69
liverwort, 12
Livy, 60
lobelia, wild, 28
lotus, 49
lovage, *14*

madder, 60
magic and superstition, 18, 20, 21, 28, 33-47, 59
maidenhair fern, 36
Majorana hortensis (sweet marjoram), *14,* 56
Mandragora officinarum (mandrake), 30, *38,* 39-41, 44, *73*
mandrake, 30, *38,* 39-41, 44, *73*
marigold, 69-70, *70,* 71
marjoram, sweet, *14,* 56
Marrubium vulgare (horehound), 34, 35, *35*
marshmallow, 19, *19*
Materia Medica (Dioscorides), 16-17
meadowsweet, 56
medicine, herbal, 9, 16-48, 55, 66, 71
- magic and, 15, 20, 21, 28, 33-48
- in modern use, 13, 28-29

Mediterranean lands, 14-16, 66
Melissa officinalis (lemon balm), *67*
Mentha piperita (peppermint), *15,* 29
Mentha spicata (spearmint), 66
Middle Ages, 9, 17-19, 43, 53, 60, 62, 66-67, 68
mint, 56, 69
Mint family, 11
mistletoe, 41
monasteries, 17, 55, 69
monkshood, 59, 59, 60
mugwort, 47, *47*
mullein, 47
mushroom, 48
musk, 36, 57
mustard, 66
myrrh, 49

Natural History (Pliny the Elder), 16
New World, herbs from, 27-28

Ocimum basilicum (basil), *15*, 49, 56
oils, volatile, 11-12, 24, 72
opium, 29
history of, 30-33
orris, 57-58
Our Lady's bedstraw, 49-50

Papaver somniferum (opium poppy), 12, 29, 30, *30*, 33, 48
Parkinson, John 20, 27
parsley, 22, 49, 66
pennyroyal, 59
peony, 12
peppermint, *15*, 29
perfume, 35, 55, 56
periwinkle, 28, 41, 42, *42*, 43, 44
Petroselimun crispum (parsley), 22, 49, 66
pewterwort, 59
Pharmacopoeia, London, 36
Pharmacopoeia, United States, 29
pimpernel, 41
plantain, 44
Pliny the Elder, 16, 60
poison hemlock, 33, 45-46, *46*, 47
poisonous herbs, 12, 24-28, 33, 39-41, 44-47, 59-60
poppy, opium, 12, 29, 30, *30*, 33, 48
potherbs, 23, 66
potpourri, 56
Primula veris (cowslip), 36, 44, 70, 71, *71*
pyrethrum, 59-60, *59*

rauwolfia, 28
religion, plants and, 27, 30, 48-50, 56
Renaissance, 19
Romans, ancient, 16, 31, 35, 48, 49, 53, 55, 61, 66, 69
rose, 36, 49, 56, 69
rosemary, 36, 48, 49, 51, *51*, 56, 59
rose water, 69
Rosmarinus officinalis (rosemary), 36, 48, 49, 51, *51*, 56, 59
rue, 22-24, *22*, 69
Rumex scutatus (French sorrel), *67*
Ruta graveolens (rue), 22-24, *22*, 69

safflower, 60
saffron, 36, 61-62, *63*, 69, 70
saffron crocus, *63*
sage, 22, 23-24, *23*, 36
St. John's wort, 12, 42, 43, *43*, 47, 75
salad burnet, *67*
salad herbs, 23, 66-68, 74
Salvia officinalis (sage), 22, 23-24, *23*, 36
Sanguisorba minor (salad burnet), *67*
Satureja hortensis (summer savory), *15*
savory, summer, *15*
scilla, 57, 58
Scotch broom, 58
scouring rush, 58-59, *58*
sesame, 29, 49
Shakespeare, William, 23, 44
simples, 21-22, 24, 28
soapwort, 57
Socrates, 46
Solomon, King, 15
Sorrel, French, *67*
southernwood, 59
spearmint, 66
spices, 10, 59, 65, 67
spikenard, 57
Stachys betonica (betony), 33-34, 35, *35*, 36
stillroom, 18, 32, *73*
stillroom book, 18-19, 36, 56, 70
Strabo, Walahfrid, 22, 34
strewing herbs, 53-54, *54*, 55, 56
summer savory, *15*
swallow-wort, 43
sweet basil, 49
sweet cypress, 56
sweet flag, 48, 54-55, *55*
sweet marjoram, 14
sweet woodruff, 53-55, *55*
Symphytum caucasicum (comfrey), *34*, 35

Tanacetum vulgare (tansy), 44, 50, *50*, 59
tansy, 44, 50, *50*, 59
tarragon, *15*
teas, herbal, 23
Teasel, 64
Theophrastus, 16, 21
thorn apple, 25, *26*, 27-28
Thutmose III (king of Egypt), 15
thyme, 56, 66
Thymus vulgaris (thyme), 56, 66
turmeric, 69
Turner, William, 20, 35

valerian, *10*, 11, 12, 56
Valeriana officinalis, *10*, 11, 12, 56
verbena, 56
vervain, 41, 47
Vinca minor (periwinkle), 28, 41, 42, *42*, 43, 44
Vinegar of the Four Thieves, 23, 35
Viola odorata (sweet violet), 56
violet, 56

witchcraft, 18, 34, 41, 44-47, 59
woad, 60, 62, *62*, 63
wolfsbane (aconite), 12, 34, 45, 59, 60
Wolsey, Cardinal, 57
woodruff, sweet, 53-55, *55*
wormwood, 44, 47, 69

yarrow, 44